D0339991

THE NEW SENIOR WOMAN

THE NEW SENIOR WOMAN

Reinventing the Years Beyond Mid-Life

Barbara M. Fleisher and Thelma Reese
Foreword by Dick Goldberg

ROWMAN & LITTLEFIELD
Lanham • Boulder • New York • Toronto • Plymouth, UK

Published by Rowman & Littlefield
4501 Forbes Boulevard, Suite 200, Lanham, Maryland 20706
www.rowman.com

10 Thornbury Road, Plymouth PL6 7PP, United Kingdom

British Library Cataloguing in Publication Information Available

Library of Congress Cataloging-in-Publication Data

Fleisher, Barbara M., 1930–
The new senior woman : reinventing the years beyond mid-life / Barbara M. Fleisher and Thelma Reese ; foreword by Dick Goldberg.
pages cm
Includes bibliographical references and index.
ISBN 978-1-4422-2356-1 (cloth : alk. paper) — ISBN 978-1-4422-2357-8 (electronic)
1. Retired women. 2. Retirement—Psychological aspects. I. Reese, Thelma, 1933– II. Title.
HQ1062.F564 2013
306.3'8082—dc23
2013018129

∞™ The paper used in this publication meets the minimum requirements of American National Standard for Information Sciences Permanence of Paper for Printed Library Materials, ANSI/NISO Z39.48-1992.

Printed in the United States of America

A woman of valor:
Give her the fruit of her hands,
And she will be praised at the gates
by her very own deeds.

—Proverbs 31:10–31

Dedicated to the memory of
our mothers, grandmothers, and aunts

—women of valor

CONTENTS

INTRODUCTION

Not long ago, we started out to write a book for and about women en approaching and experiencing life in their senior years. We found this largest and fastest-growing part of the population fascinating because, as part of it, we know that our world is light-years distant from our mothers' and grandmothers', whose roles in life were much more predictable and circumscribed than ours. We wanted to learn how other women figure out these uncharted years without role models or guideposts.

We have tried to showcase those who have figured out how to meet the challenges of these senior years constructively, women who have used retirement wisely and productively, some going on from one career to a second or third. We talk about how our new gifts of time, good health, and increased energy empower us to impact and continue contributing to society.

We narrowed our topics to those of most importance in our contemporaries' lives and in those of younger women looking to us as role models. They are addressed in narratives of women who have figured out how to maintain purpose and satisfaction in this stage of their lives, make the most of this new empowerment, maintain freedom and independence despite obstacles, downsize their lives of possessions that sometimes become overwhelming, deal with changing dynamics of the family now that the children are adults, remain a part of a changing world, cope with declining health, live beyond separation and loss, and retain intergenerational contacts. Finally, there is a summation: a gathering of the wisdom we find in one another.

Every day we see the world, with all its opportunities, challenges, diversity, new technologies, and noise crashing into our consciousness. Now we feel the need to draw together to find sisterhood and fellowship within this wider world. The old boundaries are dissolving, and women yearn to speak to, understand, and support one another.

And so we traveled to many states, personally interviewing women in their homes, in our homes, at senior centers, and at their workplaces—women in their sixties and beyond who know their lives are at a bend in the road. In most cases, the women we interviewed are identified by first name only and the city in which they live. Where they are further recognized by their writings or by organizations they have founded, we have indicated their full names. We also created a blog and heard from thousands of others across the country and around the world. We listened to their dreams and concerns, their joy and their pain.

These are their stories.

FOREWORD

Forward, ElderChicks!

"It's a new world, Golde."

That's the line from *Fiddler on the Roof* that my wife and I quote to each other whenever we encounter something for the first time. Zumba. Hotel keys that work via wifi. An app for our smart phones that does something we either never thought an app could do or wonder why anyone would want to do.

But it's not just exercise, means of entry, and technology that seem to be moving at warp speed these days. It's our whole social order.

Jihad. Gay marriage. ElderChicks. Who, thirty years ago, would have made those predictions?

Geez, we were student radicals/free love advocates in the sixties, a married couple suffused with the spirit of feminism in the seventies, and "teachable moments" parents in the eighties, and we never saw any of this coming.

I first met the authors of this delightful notion (and of this rich and delightful book), Thelma Reese and Barbara Fleisher, when I came upon their blog. It's a unique virtual spot where women sixty and beyond meet to exchange experiences, advice, and counsel for living a dynamic, rewarding senior life.

I confess: it was (platonic) love at first sight, as my work as the national director of Coming of Age involves helping people and organizations across the country think about and engage the incredible potential that older adults have, and these women not only were clearly fellow travelers, they were energetic envelope pushers, setting an incredible example and building a vibrant community.

But just what is an ElderChick, you may well ask? *I've* been asked many times, often by people who then proceed to take a crack at answering the question themselves. An older woman? Well, yes. An older woman who thinks she's got it going on? I'm sure some ElderChicks feel that way. I even encountered one woman in California who thought I was talking about poultry, as in the chronological omega to the spring chicken alpha.

I find it easiest to talk about ECs by citing examples. I was blessed to have three in my life: Aunt Tillie, Aunt Esther, and Aunt Minnie. Do the names suggest they were ElderChicks before there were ElderChicks? They all would be well over one hundred were they traversing the planet today.

But more importantly, they were high-energy, no-nonsense pioneers with an incredible sense of style—not fashion flair, though one turned out to be a true doyenne in that department.

Aunt Tillie was not a relative, but I was reared in the grits and white bread South and was taught to call my mama and daddy's friends "aunt" and "uncle." Aunt Tillie was my mother's best friend, and she got my mom—on *occasion*—to bust out of her white-gloved Victorian sensibility and, in the words of another aunt, "Auntie Mame," "Live! Life's a banquet and most poor suckers are starving to death!" She drummed that message into my mother's dear little ear starting when my mother and Aunt Tillie were in their thirties straight on through till they both were in the autumn and then winter of their lives.

Tillie moved away, but she continued to both break the mold and set the pattern. She was gutsy, a risk taker, unabashed, and incredibly generous and loving. And a role model, too. Had my mother not at least in part embraced the path that Tillie set, I am sure she would have led a much less interesting and engaged life.

Esther. Esther was a real (i.e., biologically related) aunt, my grandmother's sister. She left South Philly and became a showgirl in Chicago, appearing in *Artists and Models*. Then she came back to Philly in the 1950s and did the unheard of: she started her own business, an upscale women's clothing store using her name as its moniker (her husband, the ultimate Esquire man, reported to her, thank you very much).

When she entered her senior years, in addition to running the store, she became the family's chief mentor, offering direction and advice (occasionally even solicited) to all nephews, nieces, grandnephews and grandnieces, a few of the next generation, and assorted strangers. She cast a wide swath and a long shadow. A waif with enormous influence on how her customers should dress, how one should comport oneself socially, what one's obligations to family were—you name it. A compassionate empress.

She was outdone in charm, eccentricity, and passion for life only by *her* (and my grandmother's) sister, Minnie. The most illuminating way to talk about Minnie is to tell you about her funeral. (Full disclosure: I love funerals . . . not only because they are usually intensely emotional but also because you can learn so much at them, even if the information is presented through a "best-case scenario" filter).

At Aunt Minnie's funeral, her daughters (who were wearing caftans—are you getting a vibe?) passed around snapshots of their mom. One showed her at the beach, the apex of a human pyramid of young men. Another was of her riding a llama. Another, dancing a tango in a scene that presaged *Dancing with the Stars*. She was truly our "Auntie Mame."

The images jibed with my recollection of her. When Minnie and Esther came to my bar mitzvah, they arrived by train in the middle of the night—that's when trains got to sleepy little Southern towns in those days—and, not wanting to disturb the family, crawled into the backseat of my parents' station wagon to spend the rest of the night (Minnie was even tinier than Esther). Then the next day, Aunt Minnie, well into her seventies, entertained the out-of-town guests by performing summersaults, cartwheels, and other assorted flips and flops by the pool at the local Howard Johnson's.

Flash forward. My wife and I had been married a dozen years when Aunt Esther and Aunt Minnie came to visit us and our two little children in our suburban Philadelphia home. The house was an old ersatz Tudor without air conditioning. It was a sweltering summer day. Remember, these were very hardy souls—used to sleeping in the backseats of cars, running away to start scandalous careers, flying in the face of all manner of conventions and expectations.

They sat my wife down out of my earshot and said, "He needs to get you A/C." Not "Oh, it's hot!" Not "How can you stand it?" But an assessment of the situation, a prescription for the problem, and the person who was to be delegated to make it happen. When Esther and Minnie spoke, you listened and did what you were told, even if you were a thirty-three-year-old man and thought you might possibly maybe have a say in the matter. They weren't quite Zeus or Ramses, but they were certainly soul sisters to that deity and pharaoh.

So . . . ElderChicks are fearless, kooky, unapologetic? Not quite. More like ElderChicks are older women who sense their value, have an ability to model for the next generation, possess *joi de vivre*, and do it all their own way.

But they're also keenly aware of life's limitations and tragedies. You can't get to this point in life without experiencing and processing loss—usually, lots of it. And, lady, if you have failed to accept and process death, loss, and liabilities and lived in denial, you desperately need an ElderChick to help you with some course correction.

ElderChicks are also a manifestation of a new phenomenon: how long old age can be. We used to think you work, you live, you die, and many of us chunked life down to childhood, adolescence, young adulthood, adulthood, middle age, and old age. Then all of a sudden (well, it *seems* like all of a sudden) this period of old age, like an amoeba, bifurcated into two stages: young old age and true, or old, old age.

The young old age goes by many names: second adulthood, the encore years, the bonus years, and so on. That's now the period between middle age and true old age. Enter the ElderChicks, to function as guides like Charon did on the River Styx, but in a much more uplifting, life-affirming way. They set an example for and offer direction to women transitioning from their encore years to the next phase.

And I'm not pulling punches by calling it "the next phase." Because despite their being pioneers into this brave new world, a lot of where they're leading is uncharted territory. Our new social order hardly seems fixed.

So . . . are they making it up as they go along?

No. That's the beauty part of longevity. It can lead to accumulation—of experience, ideas—dare I say it—even wisdom. Elder-Chicks don't make it up as they go along; they take a gander at the past to see what it has to offer. Mordecai Kaplan, the paterfamilias of Reconstructionist Judaism, said, "The past has a voice, not a veto." ElderChicks of all faiths, traditions, and ethnicities are the embodiment of that dictum.

And the wonderful thing about the past, this great reservoir of experience that so many older people hold within them, is that it has depth. It has richness, it has a context against which one can

compare and contrast (a phrase from the past!) current experience . . . and the foreseeable *and* unforeseeable future.

ElderChicks offer perspective, not a recipe. They're examples,
not scripts. They provide inspiration, but they're always cognizant
that it's *you* who are at the wheel, with *your* foot on the gas and
whatever baggage *you've* accumulated piled into the trunk, as you
glide or go bumpily into the next great, challenging, or mixed-bag
act of your life.

Dick Goldberg

I

MY MOTHER'S SENIOR YEARS WERE SO DIFFERENT FROM MINE

How Should I Be in This New Age?

There are two ways of spreading light: to be
The candle or the mirror that reflects it.

Edith Wharton

Dear ElderChicks and Boomers:

In 1954, Roger Bannister did something that was never done before—he ran the distance of a mile in less than four minutes. Once he broke that barrier, other runners soon followed, and running the mile in under four minutes became routine.

We ElderChicks, in our own way, are also breaking barriers. We call ourselves *elder* because we are sixty-something and beyond. We call ourselves *chicks* because we are neither doddering nor diminished by our age as the word *hen* implies when applied to women. And we are now considering the rest of our lives. What is our place in the world?

Our mothers' senior years were so different from ours. When we were children, a woman of sixty, seventy, and well beyond was seldom seen and *never* heard. Her role was to be as invisible as

possible, sitting quietly by while younger generations marched
ahead. Like that English athlete in 1954, we ElderChicks are also
doing what has never been done before, breaking new barriers
every day. Once broken, others will quickly follow and, in fact, are
already following. This is a how-to book for today's women:

- How ElderChicks help each other master the art of a senior
  life

- How Boomers can look to ElderChicks as role models

- How ElderChicks are empowered by their new strength

- How *together* we will change attitudes about aging in our
  culture

WHAT'S GOING ON?

We started writing this book when we realized that we are reaching this stage in our lives and nothing seems familiar. We looked
around at our contemporaries and saw such a disparity between
the people who are actively engaged in life and people who are
living passively. This isn't necessarily manifested physically; some
of the most "alive" are in wheelchairs, and some of the least have
new perms, lots of makeup, and wear the latest, often youthful
fashions. And there appear to be so many of us! Were we just so
aware of our growing numbers because we had reached this age?

Our eyes opened wider, and we saw that we have, indeed,
actually entered not just a new stage, but a new era—one in
which we have a definite and newly distinct place—one in which
we represent a transition between our mothers and members of
the aging boomer generation who are fast approaching retirement
and entering *encore careers* or *encore lives*. In fact, we are the
vanguard of what is now described as the *grey tsunami*. There

really are more of us, and our numbers are growing at an unforeseen rate.

SOMETHING ELSE IS HAPPENING

As we spoke to women facing retirement, we found another
group. These are women who are much younger than traditional
retirement age, women in their fifties who are thinking about
career and lifestyle changes. They feel the need to put on the
brakes, slow down, get off the merry-go-round lives they are leading. They see the last half of their lives ahead of them and want to
make decisions based on the wisdom they have gained in the first
half. We often heard them say that decision making during the
first half had been by almost blind propulsion and the next decisions would be made with more consideration. Some of them
stayed home to raise children and are just now realizing that they
have decades looming in which to forge a new path.

Virginia F of Needham, Massachusetts, is a successful professional woman looking at retirement from this perspective. She is
young and at the top of her game. At fifty-three years of age, she
has been in the corporate workforce since her university graduation. Like many in her age group, she went to graduate school,
married, worked, rose in her profession, volunteered in the community, reared children, and now feels she is at a crossroads, a
midpoint, a possible fork in the road. The accomplishments that
her mother and grandmother might have viewed as worthy of a
full lifetime she regards as only the first half. Here is what Virginia is thinking about as she contemplates the rest of her life:

> I am vice president at a pension advisory firm, one of the
> senior people there, and I'm in charge of portfolios of invest-
> ment assets. I'm thinking of retirement. In fact, two years ago I

tried to semiretire. My husband retired early and we went on a road trip. It was fun, but after seven months of not working, I got pretty antsy. When my old company called and asked me to return, I decided to work four days a week. I am definitely at the place in my life where I'm deciding whether I want to fully retire and volunteer more—the soul-searching stage that a lot of people go through when they've had a busy career and are considering a change.

Well, knowing I have a lot of years ahead, I need to make sure that my financial resources will last. I'm in a very fortunate financial position right now. But I can't know what twists and turns my life might take. Illness? A family crisis? A bad economy? If I step off the career track now—for the second time— my chances of staying in the loop could be pretty small. I can hear the network saying, "She did it once and now she's doing it again. She must be pretty flaky!" So it's a risky business. I probably will keep churning away for another three or four years so I'll have an extra cushion of financial security.

What I would like to do is take some time off to think it all through and then get into a routine of volunteer work. The last thirty years have been hurried, harried, and breathless. There's been little time to reflect, what with my career and family responsibilities, all of which I take very seriously. My thinking at the moment is that I'd like to help kids finish high school—kids who might otherwise fall by the wayside. Graduation rates have plummeted in the last twenty years. I don't have an academic background in education, but I think I could find a path to help. I hope that the skills I've developed in the corporate world would be useful to the adolescents and their families. I know that it's not just academic tutoring that is needed. I might like to work with organizations that deal with runaway teens and offer parenting help for moms and dads. Mentoring, time management, strong role models, goal setting, support of families and community, change of expectations. These are just a few of the management issues that can make a huge difference in the future of kids at high risk for dropping out of high school and into an alternative, maybe a bad, society. I'd like to try to figure out how to deal with some of this.

Once my children left home, I began to think about these things. A lot of people don't have the luxury of choice in the matter of retirement. I, fortunately, do and feel I want to give back. Stuffing envelopes and raising money won't do it for me. I want to interact with people. I want a hands-on gig.

We have heard Virginia's sentiments not infrequently among her age peers. Hers is a generation of women who grew up wanting it all, expecting it all, and getting it all. And now they are facing the second half of their lives wanting more. They have the energy, the resources, and the will to carry on with their lives with spirit, excitement, and the enthusiasm of new beginnings.

WE'VE GOT TO TAKE CHARGE

As for us, we're beginning to recognize our own worth. We are discovering that we are role models for each other as well as for the generation that follows us. We're looking at the radical and rapid changes in the world around us and know that this extra gift of time is full of challenge and opportunity. We're recognizing that we have the time to reflect on our lives (without judging!) and to refresh and renew our own narratives. We can reassess our values and be of use in making the world around us better in ways we hadn't thought of before. Not for us is the old soldiers' vision of "just fading away." We have things to do, decisions to consider, and contributions to make.

By the way, did you know that the term *adolescence* was new in 1904? The psychologist G. Stanley Hall coined it when he described the stage in normal growth that was the focus of his research. Maybe it's time that we examine and name **our** time, which stretches past retirement from a first or even second career and presents great promise and opportunity. As the Boomers arrive in their sixties and look ahead to a longer, healthier life span than had been expected, they can look to us as a resource—for examples of what to do and, perhaps, what not to do.

OUR MISSION

Part of our mission is to transform attitudes about aging, attitudes that are already beginning to change through the observations, scholarship, and leadership emerging among the Boomers themselves. Awakening to their own looming retirement years and prospects of greater longevity, they are creating a movement that recognizes how we can be of benefit to them as well as to each other. They look ahead, and whom do they see? Us! We are the go-to and how-to people when it comes to mastering the art of a senior life.

WHAT'S HAPPENING TO OUR DEMOGRAPHICS

Age distribution has changed quite dramatically in the United States over the past sixty years. Here are some facts for you to picture:

- The US Census Bureau[1] compared age and gender distributions in 1950 and 2010. There is a huge change in proportion of the population that are middle aged and those who are sixty and older.

- In 1950, the population according to age would fit into a triangle, diminishing steadily until people would almost disappear at age eighty-plus.

- By the year 2010, however, you need to picture a rectangle because the population above age sixty has almost tripled.

- The US population as a whole doubled during this period, so the percentage of the population aged sixty-plus has increased by 51 percent, from 12.2 percent to 18.4 percent.

- Between 2000 and 2010 alone, the total population increased by 9.7 percent, from 281.4 million to 308.7 million.

- But growth over the decade was even faster for the population sixty-five and over, which grew an astonishing 15.1 percent.

- According to data compiled by the Centers for Disease Control,[2] a man reaching age sixty-five today can expect to live, on average, until age eighty-three.

- A woman turning age sixty-five today can expect to live, on average, until age eighty-five. And those are just averages.

- About one out of every four sixty-five year olds today will live past age ninety, and one out of ten will live past ninety-five.

As you can see, we are part of the fastest-growing—and largest—segment of the population: women over sixty, with a whole generation of vibrant years in our future. There are so many of us. We are a force to be dealt with. Some are widowed or never married; some live with husbands, companions, children, or alone. We've lived through the time when people who reached our ages were expected to be seen and not heard, to look their age, and to stay out of the way. Now we find ourselves surprised by our numbers, surprised by our longevity. We find we haven't used up our energy or our smarts. This turns out to be a period of self-discovery, and we have a lot to tell you.

Even the word *retirement* is fast approaching redefinition. Our title refers to "women in retirement," but some balk at being so described. Up to now, there has been a tacit understanding that those of us who were in the world of work outside the home would be given a handshake (occasionally a "golden" one) when we reached sixty-two or sixty-five. Technicalities such as the kicking in of pensions, Social Security, and Medicare aside, we're beginning to recognize this as an opportune time for very meaningful accomplishment beyond seeking amusement. We're not just sitting back or slacking off. We're shifting gears.

We've found that the same holds true for women whose work has been for family and community without a paycheck. Where there were children, they've grown. Where there were board and committee meetings, the membership may be changing but the ideas not so much. Could it be that new energy will be found in exploring new ideas? Are there new ways to find meaning through service? Women described as "not working" never were that!

Sometimes it feels as though the world was not expecting us. Unlike most "women of a certain age" of the past, we're entering our senior decades aware that we still have much to do and much to give. We've been trying to figure out how to make these years count.

WE ALL KNOW WHAT WE'RE SUPPOSED TO DO

- Keep busy!
- Stay active!
- Develop hobbies!
- Stimulate our minds!
- Exercise our bodies!

Some women remain happily connected to the world in these ways and live productively. Other women keep very busy, but for them, it is an Oscar-worthy performance at playacting, and they are constantly hiding from their discontent by filling their appointment books and panicking when an empty afternoon or evening looms, fearing that only loneliness will fill the void. Still others can't bring themselves to engage in what for them seems like fakery or meaningless busywork, and they succumb to depression.

Today women can look forward to a whole new stage of life after they retire that will likely last twenty or thirty years. This is not just a wee bit of time to spend sitting around waiting for infirmities of mind and body to do us in. This is a sizeable stage in our lives—much too long a time to be little old ladies in rocking chairs. With a bit of luck, we can expect good health, unprecedented energy, and a vital place in the world. All of us face challenges our grandmothers could hardly envision, challenges that come with an accelerating rate of change in the world and the culture around us: the Internet, the twenty-four-hour news cycle, and shifting foundations in our social institutions. But how do we do this new stage in our lives?

WHERE SHALL WE LOOK FOR ROLE MODELS?

Most of our mothers, aunts, and grandmothers didn't live as long as we do or weren't as healthy as we are and weren't as actively engaged in the world as we ElderChicks are and as you younger chicks will be. As far as the rest of the world was concerned, their productivity was pretty much over when they finished their work lives or parenting tasks. We, in this growing cohort, are walking new and uncharted paths and need to find our way without a roadmap.

The role models, it turns out, are living right among us.

They are our peers: women who have mastered the art of a senior life and are living it with flair, dignity, and a continuing sense of accomplishment. They are recognizable in every community, regardless of educational level, financial resources, ethnicity, geographical area, or family situation. We have found women to emulate among those who have married or never married, those who are widowed or divorced, those in rural and urban areas, those who are mothers or those who are childless, those who have retired, those in second careers, and those who have never worked outside the home.

In the search for meaning and inspiration in our own lives, as authors we've talked to many women from all walks of life with the aim of finding out how they manage this stage in their lives. We have seen that many of these older women are bored, depressed, regretful, and angry. They haven't found a way to deal with their excess energy, wisdom, and experience as they are being pushed out to make room for a younger generation; they often feel ignored, invisible, or patronized by younger people. Yet others clearly stand out as vibrant models for a crowning period of senior life. What do these few have to tell the rest of us—we who have already reached this stage and those of you who are approaching it?

We have taken a deep look at some of the women who seem to have figured it out—to try to discover, through their own words, how they are handling the uncharted years ahead of them. Each woman has a unique life history, yet each has faced critical events and made adjustments in its course. As you will see, despite enormous differences in their life experiences, common threads appear. It has been most rewarding to find and to interview the women you will meet in the next pages of this book.

HOW DID WE CHOOSE THE WOMEN WHOSE STORIES APPEAR?

Finding women to interview was easy. Merely reciting the title of our new project at social gatherings, senior centers we visited, discussion groups we participated in, and even doctors' waiting rooms generated intense interest among women—and quite a few men who wondered why we have made this gender restriction. We invited interested women to meet with us at what we called "Lunch and Listens" and found that they had much on their minds. Younger women told us that as they contemplate retirement, they are concerned about what their lives will hold, how they will fill their professional void or their empty nest. Some confessed that they hoped they could make a drastic change in an unfulfilled life, looking on this time as a last chance. The topic seemed to touch a nerve. Almost all could relate to the dilemmas and challenges of the senior life, and many told us of women they admire for the way they are living this stage of their lives.

Men have asked, "Why aren't we part of this book?" Not to worry, the next one will be about them. Because our experience has generally been vastly different from men's in the worlds of work, home, and the social sphere, and since gender roles have shifted so significantly during the past few decades, we decided to limit our focus to women.

We started a list.

The list became long and varied, and our interviews could fill volumes. We were looking for introspective women of varied histories who examine their lives critically. We wanted to know not only what they are doing, but why. We were turned off by women who, knowing all the answers but not the right questions, offered advice. We chose, instead, thinking women who told us what they have learned about themselves.

We examined our own ways of listening.

We recognized the difference between the kind of deep listening that begets real communication and a kind of surface listening in which the hearer is really waiting for the other person to finish so that she can say what she wishes to be heard. That kind of listening may be perfectly adequate in many social situations, but it wasn't going to work if we were to really learn from those we interviewed.

We recorded individual conversations.

Our interviews are recorded conversations. Although we had many questions in mind, they rarely had to be asked. Rather, the topics sprang forth as a natural outgrowth of reviewing women's life stories. We talked to women about how they have adapted to getting older, the events that have made them aware that they were entering a new phase in their lives. How they have coped with loss, failure, disappointment, tragedy. (And not one among us has not.) We helped them examine their attitudes toward changing mores, reorganized social structures, threats to their long-held values and belief systems. Their reactions to old passions, and their search for new interests. Their response to changed dependency and resiliency needs. The importance of friendships. The role of memories. The place of religion in their lives. As we listened, this became clear: the subjects were all theirs; the questions were ours.

We held group-thinks.

In addition to individual interviews with women whom we felt had much to teach the rest of us, we went to senior centers and held workshops—usually with twenty or more women—at which they shared their aspirations and concerns. Women found these "group thinks" particularly rewarding because the participants prompted each other to reflect on issues that hadn't risen to the surface until then. We also held "Lunch and Listens" with small groups of women at which we recorded the conversations, which were often as hilarious as they were serious. A rich sense of humor as well as a willingness to deeply and honestly reflect soon became the hallmarks of stimulating women. We began to notice a pattern.

SOMETHING ELSE HAPPENED ALONG THE WAY TO THE BOOK

Younger friends, daughters, and granddaughters were not only interested in these people but had ideas about the project that hadn't occurred to us. "Blog!" they said. And we listened. They saw the blog as a great means of communication among peers but also as a place where they, themselves, could look ahead toward their own futures. In the lives of older women, they can find role models and can envision and plan their own steps toward a fulfilling senior life. And so, with our ElderChick ears to the ground, we embraced this contemporary literary form, and ElderChicks. com was born.

Our blog, we found, was a useful way to better understand what women past mid-life are thinking and feeling. Soon a virtual community evolved. Women, it seems, want to be heard and like to communicate with each other. We gain strength from recounting our experiences. We develop wisdom when we share our views on specific topics, questions, and issues. The blog, as it turned out, was a rich lode for us to mine in order to gain insight into the minds and hearts of senior women—and younger women as well. Enriching all of our experience have been the contributions to the blog of many self-described "ElderChicks-in-training," women who expect the future to be as productive as the past.

Most loved the moniker *ElderChicks*. They liked the humor, they liked the logo, they liked the whole idea of gathering together and talking openly about aging as a natural process rather than as if aging were a contagious disease to be somehow hidden.

A few cringed. Why did they cringe? The use of the term *elder* irritated them. But isn't that what we are? *Elder* rather than *younger*?

IT'S TIME TO CHANGE THE CULTURE

Why is "elder" a pejorative term?

Why deny that we've gotten to this point successfully? The culture around us needs to be changed, edified, helped to reevaluate. And we're trying to do just that. We are presenting evidence that during the *elder* part of our lives, women in the second half of their lives remain as bright, energetic, involved, and funny, albeit wiser and more interesting because of the experiences we've lived through on our way here.

Others objected to "chicks."

"Cutesy" or even "demeaning" was heard from a few. We didn't see it that way. The twelve-year-old **Emma B** of Palo Alto, California, who designed our logo, saw it just as we did, putting an about-to-hatch egg in place of the *o* in dot.com. She saw us as people in a time of renewal and reinvention. True, *chicks* can be a cheeky reference to women, but we like this double meaning of women finding a time for renewal.

It's time to take control.

The women whose stories we have chosen to include in this book, though very different, seem to have at least one common thread: they have taken control of their lives. They are not drifting aimlessly into their golden years, expecting to sit out their dotage watching the young carry on the business of managing the world pretty much, they hope, within the safe traditions handed down to them. On the contrary, the women we have interviewed are still very much in the game. We know that this book provides role models for all women approaching and beyond mid-life who look ahead to decades of meeting life's opportunities and challenges.

WHAT WE HAVE FOUND IN THESE STORIES

Like any other stage of life, this new stage benefits from preparation. The women in these stories have figured out that there are goals to be set, plans to be implemented, and checks to be made on whether they're accomplishing what they've set out to do. They didn't enter adulthood without thoughts about job and family. They didn't enter their working years without a general plan for what they hoped to accomplish in work and leisure. They didn't enter parenthood or marriage without expectations about how to fulfill their roles as parents and homemakers. And neither have they entered this stage in their lives without thoughts, plans, expectations, projections about the future, and resiliency to adapt to unforeseen changes when life throws them curves.

Here's where preparation has the biggest payoff.

With open minds, and not sure of what we would find, we began our search for role models. None of the "how-to" or advice books for the elderly addressed what we were looking for: people who are truly mastering the art of a senior life, whose own individual examples would help us find our own individual answers. We've learned that each of these women is benefiting from the unexpected gift of years in learning who she really is, in reflecting, renewing, and reassessing her own narrative. The women we met are choosing to remain in the world as participants in life, not mere consumers and observers. Despite, and sometimes because of, difficult challenges life has presented, they are often surprised at how very good they are finding this time. Here, in their own words, are their stories. We hope you will learn from them as we have.

The science of mastering this stage in our lives is up to our doctors. The art is up to us.

2

SO NOW I'M RETIRED

How Do I Fill My Days So I Feel Good about Myself at Night?

The trick is in what one emphasizes. We either make ourselves miserable, or we make ourselves strong. The amount of work is the same.

—Carlos Castaneda

This is the challenge, the dilemma, the fear.

It strikes terror in people contemplating retirement, fosters anger in those who sense they are no longer valued, creates guilt in those who fear they are filling their days with aimless puttering.

"In youth the days are short and the years are long. In old age the years are short and the days long." It has been more than three hundred years since a great Russian statesman and thinker, Nikita Panin, observed this. Most of us have the privilege of many more years to look forward to than did Panin's contemporaries, but the sentiment still holds true.

As we went around the country interviewing people, individually and in small groups that we called "Lunch and Listen," we found many who were not willing to confront their feelings of anger, unease, or frustration or even to recognize this underlying question. Scratching the surface, however, we found that this was the number one issue for many of the women who claimed they were busier in retirement than ever, that with all they now do, they can't imagine how they ever had time to work professionally or as homemakers. In actuality, when they did confront the issue, they realized that life was taking on a treadmill quality where busyness was the goal and discontent was the reality. They indeed recognized the possibility that many healthy years might lie ahead of them with little they valued consuming their time and spirit.

Here is a case in point. Let's let **Honey A** of Pittsburgh, Pennsylvania, tell her own story:

> *What is their secret? For those who are writing on your blog, life seems to be treating them well. They are justifiably proud of their work before and after retirement and pleased with what's happening in their world. Am I the only one whose life is not going well?*
>
> *My seventy-five years have been quite ordinary. I grew up in a beautiful house with a father, a sister, and a psychotic mother, married at nineteen to escape, had three wonderful children, got divorced, had a few affairs, remarried happily, and was widowed three years ago. Nothing unusual so far. Baggage? Bad hip and eye issues, but I'm coping.*
>
> *I worked in the beauty business for a while, which I loved, but my career has mainly encompassed advertising and public relations, first for Gimbels, as a copywriter, then the Jewish Federation, and later as the assistant news editor of the Jewish newspaper in Pittsburgh, where I live. I was lucky to interview celebrities like Elie Wiesel, a difficult man, and Isaac Bashevis Singer, a sweetheart, as well as many local people who, in their own way, had also done extraordinary things.*

Ezer Weizmann, son of Chaim Weizmann, was the first famous person who came my way. I was sent in a hurried fashion to see him and had no time to get background information in the paper's "morgue." Because I was nervous, in my questioning I demoted him from the general that he was to colonel and was immediately gleefully corrected by the religion editor of the daily paper. The general kindly asked if this was my first interview and when I said that it was, he slanted the entire hour to me, giving me my first byline. Sadly, I recently read of his death.

What are your plans now? How are you spending your days? You have so much talent. Are the bad hip and the cataracts limiting your activities?

Other than solving my medical problems, I have no plans at the moment, and this disturbs me. Hip surgery looms as well as cataract removal—the evil twins. Gone are the fun days of songwriting for revues and hilarious tap-dancing classes.

I have always been busy, always had a project. At the end of the day I always had that satisfying feeling of having accomplished something. If it wasn't lyrics for a show I was working on, it was an ad or an article for a magazine or newspaper. I was creative and I felt alive. But now I'm drifting like one of those balloons running out of air, hitting the ground occasionally and getting a little bounce, but basically without direction. Freedom is not as exhilarating as I had imagined.

I am somewhat embarrassed to put this message out there. I blush at what I've said but I'm hopeful that you happy and achieving ElderChicks can teach me how to live this part of my life. Did you lay your plans well in advance? Have you always known where you were going, or are you just lucky, born under the right sign?

Please tell me their secret so I can find the answer to my dilem-
ma. Don't let me down. I'm counting on you to help me get my
mojo back.

We welcomed Honey's reluctance to express her negative feelings
about retirement. She affirmed our belief that women may need a
safe place to share concerns and apprehensions as well as success
in adjusting to retirement. For so many of us, even while being
grateful for reaching this stage in our lives with faculties intact
and in good health, the feelings are mixed.

Lucia Blinn of Chicago, Illinois, is also conflicted her about
retirement. Here is her very compelling poetic expression of
these feelings.

This Is Not Working[1]

You think this is easy? This daily reinventing
that I might catch the driverless
coach and find a seat? The cosmic joke,
another in a humorless series, is that working is
work and not is bliss. A lie of the patent variety.
Remember the New Yorker cartoon?
Failure: the bum on a desert isle.
Success: the man behind a desk.
Failure failed to show the effort
in not showing up. Success is a snap.
Get up, get dressed, get going,
do what they say, take home the pay.

Blair said the hardest part was waking up
and hearing the fire bell only there was no fire.
Only there is, Blair, and we are not invited.

Which is the problem. Much as I craved the
blaze that year after motherhood
this is how it is now. My rooms are not my rooms

between eight and six. Dust bunnies
yearn for privacy. The machine itches to answer.
The refrigerator groans: can't I chill in peace? Let them.
Give me the moans and nervous laughter of
downtown souls who pirouette their papers
in that anxious ballet.

You didn't retire, you cashed in, they said. So, yes,
right on schedule, I am taking the long walks and
reading the long books that, until the minute I got to them,
sounded like the goal of holies.

So this is how it is to be a senior before the junior is cold.
This is the shrieking beneath the nursing home rocking.
Wait a minute. I wasn't finished.

But don't get the impression that all we heard as we talked with women around the country was discontent, anger, and guilt, or the uncertainty of not quite knowing how to be in this new stage in their lives. On the contrary, this odyssey to find women who are aging with flair, dignity, and spirit was a joyful journey, full of examples for all of us and filled with the realization that we can learn from each other how to make the most of this gift of time.

Joan L of New York, New York, told us that when retirement was looming, she, like many others, was terrified at the thought. She likes to wake up in the morning knowing that her day is planned, that it will hold interest, and that she will accomplish something. As a high school English teacher, her identity had always been clear and her days filled with purpose. What would take its place after the school bell stopped ringing for Joan? The answer eluded her and, in fact, the first year of retirement turned out to be a terrible drag. So she and her husband made a major decision: they moved from Long Island, New York, to Manhattan—a distance of only twenty-two miles geographically but really a chasm away. Lawrence was where she had grown up; in Manhattan she was anonymous. She and her children had even attended the same schools. Lawrence people do not drop in on you once you move to Manhattan. "In a way," she said, "I didn't leave home until I was past fifty."

Joan felt lonely in Manhattan during the first year. But as often happens when you reach out, many grabbed her hand, and she ultimately created a new and rewarding life. She looked for places to volunteer her time.

New York is harried and hurried. It's hard to get noticed. How did you reach out to people? Where did you find a focus for your skills and interests?

My first foray into the world of volunteering was at the Metropolitan Museum of Art, where, knowing I had the skills for it, I decided to become a docent. What I found was that the art world was not waiting for me. There was already a long line of wannabe volunteers. Besides, I was not a big contributor to the museum, nor was I involved in their fund-raising. They suggested that I try to find work in the gift shop. Not what I had in mind.

I began to pursue my interests. I signed up for classes, lectures, joined a physical fitness facility. Through these activities, I met women who were often new retirees or women who, like me, had recently moved to the city. We both needed and enjoyed each other and soon formed a nucleus of friends which also included our husbands.

I know you do lots of volunteer work. What are some of your favorites?

I've always felt a strong need to contribute to other people's lives. My first volunteer work was at the Federation of Jewish Philanthropy, matching people to agencies which were seeking volunteers. It was there that I found and decided to match myself to an agency that helps Russian immigrants with their English. This turned out to be perfect for me. I found the Russian émigrés very bright and well educated but at a loss in a strange country with a new ideology. One of the new arrivals had been an aerodynamics engineer, another an astrophysicist, and there they were, working in a hotel. I got to know people quite well and often helped them outside the agency. I took them on tours of New York, helped them deal with their family problems. One woman had married an American soldier who was abusing her. He had kicked her in the stomach when she was pregnant, had put a hot iron on her belly, and she ended up naked at a shelter. I wound up being her advocate. I went to court with her, wrote persuasive letters in her behalf, and raised enough money for her to hire a lawyer. I loved helping people negotiate their new worlds. But then the agency moved to Brooklyn. I didn't want to travel daily to Brooklyn, so I decided to find another project. I still get letters from some of the people I had worked with.

I am always on the lookout for rewarding volunteer activities. I have worked at the Lighthouse, tutoring blind students to help them pass the New York state high school equivalency tests. I have also been involved in politics.

Tell me how you got involved in politics. I know you are a woman of strong opinions and like to follow through when you decide a cause is worth promoting.

Chatting with a stranger at a bus stop, I found my way into the Wesley Clark campaign. He lost, but I now was in the cross-hairs of political workers who kept me in the loop. I worked for Kerry and then for Obama.

One of the things I did was organize a yard sale fund-raiser. Actually, it was two of the things because we did it twice. We converted the outside of our house into a marketplace. We set up tables where we sold merchandise and also had booths to register people to vote. Who can resist a neighborhood yard sale? We posted signs in neighboring streets. Many people wanted to help. Networks of people took on various responsibilities. Some arranged for goods to be donated, some set up the tables, tons of people showed up to buy. Enthusiasm for this project snowballed, and my porch, garage, and basement were overflowing with items for sale. Volunteers were out on the streets leafleting the neighborhood, and yard sale day turned into a happening.

Between the two "market days" we raised close to $17,000. Maybe this isn't a lot of money when you think of the big donors to super PACs who wrote single huge checks, but this was a grassroots endeavor, and I feel that its political worth far exceeded the money that was raised. The enthusiasm that was evident all day long impacted everyone who worked, sold, and bought—and we became a legion of voters!

So these are some of my retirement activities. I like to throw myself into a project, conceive it, organize it, follow it through to completion, and then move on to the next. I'm no longer terrified of retirement. I love the freedom and the variety in my life. We are financially secure, we are healthy, and I know that new and exciting projects will always find their way into my world.

As Joan reflected on her retirement, she added this:

Our talk stirred memories of walking a carriage as a young mother and hoping that I would meet another mother on the way. Even someone I didn't like would do as long as I could talk to someone. I've heard similar thoughts from other moms, young and old. The beginning of retirement was very similar. Suddenly one is isolated and hoping to find company and, like a young mother, must push herself to find people and activities that work in her new role. It's an interesting cycle.

Joan is a coper. After all, retirement is just another challenge that we face in life. We call upon all our resources, including strength, resiliency, and humor. The added thing about retirement is that we also can throw experience and wisdom into the mix because we're older and have lived longer. Why are some people able to master the art more elegantly than others?

Here is another of many stories by women who have welcomed this stage of life with élan. Of course, what they have is something special: the imagination to see possibilities and the energy to seize opportunities.

Meet **Hanne Mintz** of Los Angeles, California:

Now seventy and living in Los Angeles, also having left the suburbs, Hanne has always been a very high-energy person. She was already licensed at twenty-one to teach English, German, and French in her native Sweden when she had a summer job as a concierge in a Stockholm hotel:

> *I looked across the lobby, saw this man, and my heart skipped a beat. Two days later we decided to get married. My father and stepmother hoped it wouldn't last, but we did—and it did. I was twenty-two and Bert was fifteen years older, an American there on a consultation with his engineering company for the Swedish air force. When I came to America I had no teaching credentials, and foreign languages were not in demand in the schools. When I looked for jobs, the first and sometimes only question asked was, "Can you type?" The answer was no; I had never learned in my academics-only schooling, and I had thought it might pigeonhole me into jobs I wouldn't want.*

Two days! Have you always been so decisive?

> *I guess so. My first job lasted about a day and a half. I was a "figure consultant" at an early version of a woman's gym. I had to walk around in black tights with a white overblouse, a belt to show off my waist, and high heels. It was so demeaning, and*

I felt so sorry for the women coming in. It's almost like retribution that I look like those women today!

I soon found Berlitz, the language school, walked in, introduced myself, and showed them my credentials from Sweden. They looked them over and asked me if I could type. This time I said "Of course." I went home in a panic and asked my husband if he could show me how. He couldn't, but a friend had a typewriter, which I found very confusing because the letters were in an unfamiliar pattern. But I managed to learn. That's what gets a lot of us through life—instead of saying "no" to what we realize a lot of other people can do, being cocky enough to say "yes" and learning how. Now I teach my staff that whenever someone calls and asks if we can do something, "Get the information, say 'Yes,' and then tell me: 'Okay, Boss, I said yes, now what do we do?'" We then get together, have a powwow, and figure out how to do it. It just takes will and creativity.

How did you reach the point at which you have a staff to direct?

While my children were small, I established myself as a free-lance translator and later a language specialist for the Los Angeles Superior Court. About 140 languages are spoken in the county, and I recognized the need for honest brokers who could really represent what non-English speakers were saying. With no certification in translation required by the county when I started, the need was evident. From my own experiences, good and bad, I could see what needed to be done and how to properly run an organization, both in terms of the service we could provide and how to treat staff—aware that everyone deserves to know they are valued for the work they do and the people they are. I was able to start my business twenty-one years ago. Now Paragon Language Services has about eleven in-house staff and some three hundred independent contractors we hire to cover about eighty languages as a full-service language bureau with international clients.

My life is very full. [You will read more about Hanne later.]
Here in the city I also make time for IKAR, a Jewish commu-
nity that is more than a congregation. It is an expression, for
me and others, of a way of life that inspires and allows us to try
to make the world better. I work with the groups that provide
food for those who are hungry and tutor homeless children.

A widow for the past five years, Hanne's office is only about a
mile from home, a nice walk with her dog, who accompanies her
to work.

This is not to say that we all have, or are fortunate enough to
have, Joan's or Hanne's health and energy.

Shirley L of Philadelphia, Pennsylvania, in her mid-eighties, is
another woman we interviewed in our quest for role models. Shirley plays tennis twice a week and goes to the gym on the other
days, still works at the art dealership she and her late husband
founded (which she now runs online), and volunteers regularly.

She was interviewed recently by a young writer for a national
organization's publication. The magazine, which included a piece
about www.ElderChicks.com, was looking for physically active
seniors. With Shirley's permission, we referred the writer to her.
The first question was, "What would you say to someone your age
if you saw her just sitting on her sofa and watching TV?" Shirley's
spirited reply was, "I'd ask her if she's comfortable." Reporting
back on the interview to me, Shirley said, "It's not for me to judge
what someone else can or *ought* to do, nor is it the reporter's."

This nonjudgmental attitude toward people endears Shirley to
others and ensures that they seek her company and her counsel.
Shirley is a positive person—neither angry, nor depressed, nor
bitter. As a result, she does not feel ignored, patronized, or diminished by her senior status. Here is an excerpt from our interview
with her:

Does anything make you aware that you're aging?

I've been very blessed with generally good health and to have the financial ability to do most of the things I want to, such as travel. I've never really been aware of growing old—except when I look in a mirror or catch a glimpse of myself in a window. Sometimes I see a younger woman wearing something I think is really attractive and catch myself as I realize I can no longer wear what she's wearing; I think, "Your body isn't shaped like that anymore. You no longer have a waistline!" I know it sounds weird, but I have never thought of myself as old.

Do you feel that young people regard you differently now that you're in your eighties?

The only time I have felt—and didn't like—an attitude from young people toward my age was at the gym. I don't like being asked if I need help getting up. For a long time I didn't tell my age. But I can't think of an instance where people have said I was too old, even if they thought it.

As we age, unfortunately, from illness and death, we have fewer people to share our activities. How important are your friendships and social life?

As a single woman, the Cosmopolitan Club (a professional women's club in Philadelphia, Pennsylvania, in existence since 1928) has become very important to me. It's a place I can go where I don't feel I have to have an escort. I can hear interesting speakers and have dinner with interesting people who have become my friends. I've worked on several committees. It's a comforting feeling for any woman who is alone to have a place like Cheers—where everybody knows your name. I also buy tickets for shows and concerts so I can invite someone I don't get to see much otherwise. I find that even if I don't like the show, it's an opportunity to see someone I like.

I've also found that I now socialize with people I've known for many years but didn't find appealing or interesting years ago. Maybe it's because we have more in common as we grow older. Maybe I can't be as choosy as I used to be.

Most women dread getting old. Do you see any advantages to being older?

I just think I know so much more. And listen! I'm not above using my age now when it's helpful to get what I want. I used to be subservient in dealing with other people. I felt that I had to agree with people in order for them to like me. That's really changed. I've become more self-satisfied and independent in my thinking and more assertive in dealing with people.

Jane Stevens of Davis, California, is almost sixty-five, and she feels empowered. We asked her what she's thinking about as she contemplates the second half of her life.

I see possibly three decades ahead of me, and I feel I have a lot to do. This stage in my life is a real starting point for the work that I'm doing. I'm a journalist, and that hasn't changed. But what I'm now focusing on is more mission driven than story driven. I've been a health science and technology journalist until now. In the current climate, journalism mostly needs to be entertainment, but it can also be useful. About a year ago I realized it was most important to me to focus my journalism on being more useful than entertaining. My definition of useful journalism is that people will take action after reading the story. These days, if a story reaches a lot of people, it's probably more entertaining than useful. I'm taking advantage of the new technology to define journalism and my role as a journalist in a very different way.

I'm seeking to create a safe place and a trusted source for people to tell their stories and to connect with each other in a way that they can make use of the information that we can

provide to each other. My role is to serve this growing commu-
nity by digging out the facts that lead to solutions.

Tell me more about this community. What connects them? What interests do they have in common?

The community is concerned with people who have suffered adverse childhood experiences (ACE). This community has come together because of their interest in developments in four areas of research that have converged in a perfect storm: epidemiology, neurobiology, epigenetics, and biomedicine. They are bound by their concern that toxic stress is really, really bad for fetuses, babies, children, teens, adults, communities, countries. The ACE studies contain overwhelming evidence that toxic stress harms us all. Changes in brain structure as well as their relevance to adult diseases have been documented in these studies conducted at Kaiser Permanente in collaboration with the Centers for Disease Control and Prevention. Because of it, children can't learn, can't focus, don't trust adults, have trouble with authority, grow up to be troubled adults. Toxic stress includes all the usual suspects: sexual, verbal, and physical abuse; abandonment by a parent; observing a murder; an incarcerated parent; alcoholism and drug abuse in the household; and so on.

When you say you want to report stories that are more useful than entertaining, whose stories are these?

As a result of all this research there has now developed a community of people across the spectrum who are introducing trauma-informed practices into their institutions to try to prevent the harmful effects of toxic stress, based on the research that has come out of these four areas. There are now people in schools, courts, prisons, hospitals, mental clinics, businesses, you name it, who are configuring evidence-based practices to change how our systems work. In one city, there was a 40 percent drop in school expulsions and an 80 percent drop in school suspensions when a group instituted some of these evidence-based practices. Some of these situations and solutions are described in ACE² studies. This is happening in thousands of schools. A handful of communities have started trauma-informed task forces and ACE task forces. They are scattered across the country, and I am trying to bring them together.

How are you doing that? If I were having a problem, how might I find out about ACEs?

I've developed two sites on the Internet. ACEsConnection.com is the social network where 830 people—it's growing every day—connect and exchange ideas. Pediatricians, social workers, politicians, attorneys, criminal justice, are all part of the ACEs community. The site contains links to evidence-based practices, resources, and research so that the community can keep up to date on scientific knowledge as it impacts destructive behavior due to toxic stress. This is a worldwide movement. I have another site called ACEsTooHigh.com, which is a straight news site. This is where the stories appear so that I can start informing the general public about trauma-informed practices. I've also started writing for the Huffington Post. Other sites pick up my stories, and I don't often know about it until someone tells me. That's the nature of media on the Internet these days. Some stories take on a life of their own.

The one piece of this that tells me that this is a very different phase of my life is that I'm self-funding all this. I just decided to go for it. No program like this existed before I started one. It's a new social movement. Our institutions need to change so that we can do everything to stop traumatizing already traumatized people and do everything we can to prevent toxic stress. I didn't know if this would work, but there are already 830 members. All found my site by word of mouth, no outreach whatsoever. Now I'm going for funding because I can now say,

"Look! People need this, they want this, people are making use of this, it's making a difference."

Good luck to Jane. She is empowered at this stage of her life, not diminished. She is one more person who is not content to sit back and say, "Someone should do something about this!"

Barbara S of Bryn Mawr, Pennsylvania, is a woman who feels good about her life at eighty-three. She, her son, daughter, and son-in-law live in a large, old, comfortable house in the Philadelphia suburb where she grew up. Her husband died peacefully at home two years ago, at ninety-one, after a long illness. Barbara has always been a caregiver, from her girlhood, when her father relied on her help with her three younger siblings and mentally ill mother, to her dedication to her own blended family of grown children and grandchildren, never differentiating between "his" and "hers."

She fought all the way to the state capital for help when her son, now in his early fifties, exhibited the behaviors later labeled "autism" and she had read everything she could find on his condition. At sixty-two, she took a job at a day care that lasted seventeen years. She also began to volunteer at a community senior center. A seamstress after high school, she has, for the past twenty-one years, taught one sewing class and one quilting class a week there. She still loves to cook, bake, and garden.

Her own words illuminate Barbara's inner strength and spirit.

About her classes:

My classes are quite diverse. Many Latino, black, and Filipino women attend and are all comfortable together. I think when we get older, we're more willing to say the things we really feel. This bunch of women have been around each other, doing things together, and they know that they can speak frankly and nobody's feelings are going to be hurt. This wasn't always true when we were all younger, growing up and raising our children.

Most of my students are in their late seventies and eighties. Two are in their nineties. They don't do much sewing, but boy do they talk! I just love it. My father always raised us to accept people as they are and not pass judgment about how they live their lives. Their sewing ability goes from zero to ten, and I love being there with all these different people from different backgrounds. One woman is a millionaire. Some of the talk is out of sight and off the wall. But it seems to be honest and from the heart. They talk about their ex-husbands, their children, their flirtations. Nothing is off limits. The class has gotten a name: "If you want a good laugh, go into sewing class." Most of the women live alone. Ethel has been in my class since I formed it. She's ninety-three. Since she had to move nearer to her grandson, she drives from her house to Belmont Hill to get the bus to come to the center. That's how important the socialization is. For those few hours they are there, they are happy and involved in something creative and good.

About gardening: What is so satisfying?

The hands in the dirt, planting seed, and watching it come to life. Then cleaning up in the fall. I enjoy cleaning up in the fall as much as I do planting. I love taking part in all the cycles of life.

About depression:

Sometimes I get depressed. I think everybody does. I walk. It's almost like clearing my head. I don't watch TV much, even though it's on. I'm always sewing, knitting, crocheting, or reading a book.

About family:

Barbara remains immersed in the lives and achievements of her educated and accomplished children and grandchildren. She cared for her bedridden husband at home. In his last years, the family moved him to a first-floor room where he could be more involved in household goings-on. She spoke of a granddaughter who stopped into the house with a little boy as we were talking together:

> My granddaughter is legally blind and is doing amazingly well living on her own. That's her little foster son. A friend of hers knew this little boy. His mother was in jail and the grandmother just could not take four children, only three. Jasmine is taking care of the boy until his mother gets out. The giving thing is in the family.

There are so many ways to give and so many benefits, according to the women we've met. Here's a sampling of the ways some people combine volunteering with other pastimes or skills in short-term or long-term experiences.

Marylen Oberman of Ann Arbor, Michigan, has found a way to share a skill, lend an ear and a hand, and connect with young people at the same time:

> A friend and I are volunteer mentors of teenage girls at a middle school in Florida. Our mentees are girls with lots of anxiety in their lives, very little privilege—and more school "issues" than most. It's not that they think their lives are tougher than other kids' lives. It's that they don't often know another way that life can be.
>
> The girls sought us out. Mentors were offered to them by a psychologist at the school, during school time, in a one-on-one

situation. We're not there to tutor, nag, or judge their behavior. We're not there to tell them to go to school, do their homework, and play nice. We are there to be trusted, stable adults in their often chaotic lives.

So what do you talk about with an African American teenager when you are a white grandmother wintering comfortably in Florida?

We believed we needed to focus on something external and nonthreatening. We decided to teach them to knit. And did they ever learn fast! We chat, each alone with our mentees because the time we spend with them is private. While we sit and knit, we talk to them about ourselves: things that are of concern to us, things that we do, our own grandchildren's anxieties and how that affects us. What we find is that as we open ourselves to them, giving them the respect and dignity they deserve as human beings, they also open up to us. I think they like to be with us! On the appointed days, we find them waiting for us, knitting in hand, before we arrive. And—for a bonus they always seem to attend school on the days they are expecting us. This project involves connecting several dots:

- *Longboat Key, Florida: We hear about a project called* Care Squares: Empowering Women One Stitch at a Time. *Its purpose is to present afghans to women as they leave Hannah House, a halfway house in Philadelphia, where formerly incarcerated women learn the skills they need to reenter society.*

- *Villanova, Pennsylvania: We contact Margie Rosenberg, who started the project, and she sends several kits of yarn, needles, stitch counters, instructions, and a beautiful letter explaining the scope and purpose of the project. We are greatly impressed with her project and the professional way she puts the materials together.*

- Sarasota, Florida: *We show the materials to the counselor at the school where we volunteer and ask to start an after-school knitting club and take on the* Care Squares *project. Our young knitters are excited about making the afghan and stay after school to knit squares. Although our mentees are excited about the project, the club gets off to a slow start. Are the other kids a little suspicious? Who are those women with the gray hair? They don't know yet that we are Elder-Chicks! Upbeat, involved, and interested in their world. One day a boy stops us in school and asks if he can learn to knit. Other kids stop by and show lots of interest. None of the girls thinks it is strange for a boy to be knitting. Isn't it great that gender stereotypes are changing?*

- Philadelphia, Pennsylvania: *With the help of other women who have offered to make squares, the afghan was completed. The girls in the club arranged the squares in a pattern which they designed and helped sew together. The completed afghan was presented to the women in the halfway house. Much hugging, crying, and crowing. We showed pictures of the girls, along with notes of support they had written. Can't wait 'til next year for the next project!*

The After School Knitting Club is well under way now and in its second year. This year they knitted articles for the premature baby unit at Sarasota Memorial Hospital. During our next year we are planning that each returning girl will take on a "little sister" in the school, and who knows where the new format will take us! Our big payoff for this project is the kids and their attitudes:

- *They love the idea that they are doing something for others who are in need of support.*

- *Their thinking and their reach is now going beyond this activity.*

- *They have suggested additional projects for next year.*

- *They've learned what the word* empowerment *means.*

Before she retired, **Betty N** of El Cerrito, California, was a psychiatric social worker. Music also played a large part in her life. She was a music therapist, taught music to children, and taught piano at Northwestern University. Following this busy career, she was not one to opt out of the world.

I have found in the past twenty-five-plus years since I retired that volunteering is a great way to interact with many people of many ages. I have actively applied my energies to issues I was excited about . . . and you know what? I've met many others who share my interests. Over the years I have volunteered in a wide range of activities, including health care, music, and the arts—and have met some terrific people doing so. I strongly believe that if you don't need to work, you owe the community where you have chosen to live your energy, your time, and your talents. Right now I'm off to work at a festival on the Fourth of July.

To which **Jane W** of Santa Rosa, California, responded:

That's wonderful for you, Betty, and all the lives you enrich. When my Uncle Israel retired, he began to volunteer by delivering Meals on Wheels. He was an inspiration to me as he continued his commitment well into his nineties. Whenever I'd say something like, "I bet you light up the room when you make a delivery," he'd modestly say, "Nah, I get so much more back."

Dorothy C of Jenkintown, Pennsylvania, volunteers through RSVP (Retired Senior Volunteer Program):

In my new assignment I'm visiting a ninety-year-old woman who lives alone and is very alert. She was never married and has no children, so she's essentially alone. She's quite excited to have a visitor. But I feel I'm getting as much as I'm giving. After I saw how absolutely immaculate her apartment was and learned she does all her own cleaning, I went home and scrubbed my place. I guess I see her as a mentor on healthy aging.

Martha M of Philadelphia, Pennsylvania, is always thinking of ways to fit more into her schedule and is thinking of forming a group like this one at the condominium where she lives:

We attended a large dinner party recently at a friend's house, and there were two people in the kitchen (a husband and wife) who helped with the party preparation, served cocktails, dinner, washed dirty dishes, pots and pans, straightened up afterwards, and generally lent a hand to the hosts by lightening their work load. They were a retired couple in their early seventies who happened to live in the same development as our friends. The couple had formed the "GivingGroup" with several other friends, in which the aim was to help out, charge money for their labor, and then donate the money to the charity of their choice. Rather than just writing a check to contribute to an organization, this group chooses to help people with their time. For example, they babysit, garden, run errands, organize lives, iron, sew, whatever is needed—and often at rates that are more in keeping with what the people can afford than what they would have to pay others.

The GivingGroup couple that I met always chooses to help at parties and donate their earnings for the evening to the American Cancer Society. At the end of that evening, the hosts wrote a check to the Cancer Society and the GivingGroup couple mailed it in. The fees are very reasonable for their services, and they are kept busy for as often as they choose to be. This helps people who normally might have to forgo the activities if it weren't for the GivingGroup because they couldn't afford the necessary help. Everybody wins: people get the help they otherwise can't afford, a worthy charity gets money, the GivingGroup volunteers get a good feeling in their hearts.

Andrea C of Portland, Oregon, not only finds the opportunity to care for her mother pleasurable but says that it presents a gift that enables them to move far beyond a troubled past relationship:

> *But even if she were not my mother, if she were another elder who couldn't do things for herself, if there were no personal history to either overcome or expand on, it would still be an exquisite experience because an elder has so much to give, contains so much history, knows so much, and has loved and cared and learned things far beyond what anyone else has to offer. It would be foolish to pass up the opportunity to spend time with anyone over seventy who has a grip on life and wants to share it.*

In Chicago, Illinois, **Lois Roelofs's** professional life was all about giving, as a nurse and as a professor of nursing, while taking care of home, husband, and children. She thought that when she retired she'd "take care of herself for a change."

> *But of course that doesn't work when giving is in your blood! So, after working ten years on a memoir[3] of my nursing career, when my husband suggested we donate all proceeds to Trinity Christian College, where I used to teach, I was delighted! Knowing that many of us will wake up someday to see the caring face of a nurse—whether or not we want to!—I'm happy to smooth the way for nurses in their educational process.*

Marsha P of Bala Cynwyd, Pennsylvania, told us:

> *I love this idea of combining the writing, the teaching, and the giving. It makes such sense . . . life coming full circle . . . integrating all of the pieces . . . all of the parts of oneself . . . this is an inspiration to me! Thank you for enabling us to share this.*

Brenda S approaches the rest of her life from a different perspective. She says she looks back to look forward. Brenda has

lived in Philadelphia for thirty years. Like many native New York-
ers, she never learned to drive when she lived there. She attended
Washington Irving High School ("where Claudette Colbert
went"). Brenda was interviewed at a senior center in central Philadelphia. This is far from her home, but she chose to join with a
friend rather than join one nearer her house, where she lives
alone since her husband's death twenty years ago and the gradual
moving out of her six children as they grew up but remained
nearby.

The ninth of ten children, Brenda says:

> My mother was my hero. She died a few months short of one
> hundred, still able to recite poems she learned in elementary
> school. She lived on her own until she was ninety-five and her
> other daughters insisted she live with one of them.

> Mother taught me life lessons I didn't realize I was learning at
> the time. Besides the regular housekeeping and cooking skills,
> she arranged with the local bank manager for me at age eleven
> to make deposits and withdrawals as needed.

> I think it's important to convey our experiences to other gener-
> ations. When I was young I hung out with my friends, but I
> also spent a lot of time with older people. It really helped me to
> learn about the negative things they went through—and the
> things that I could avoid! Now my seventeen-year-old grand-
> daughter has asked if she can come live with me. I said, "Of
> course." At one time I would have asked all about why. Now I
> know enough to wait for her to tell me.

Brenda had been working as an aide at a preschool and decided to
retire when she recently turned sixty-five. She loved the children
and the work but says she doesn't have time to miss it because she
looks forward to doing so many other things, things she hasn't had
time to do until now.

I'm not retired; I'm refired! I signed up for computer class. I want to learn guitar and drums. I have some college credits and at least want to complete an associate's degree. I have some ideas for children's books; I know what they like and need to hear. I'll continue doing sacred and liturgical dance and learn to drive! I do know God helps us.

Brenda's life is guided by her curiosity and her faith. She throws herself into activities that are outside the physical perimeter of her existence. She is more concerned with what other people do, need, and think than the limited walls of her house, her own ectoplasm.

Not many of us can remember the flu epidemic that swept the world in 1918, killing an estimated fifty million people, more than World War I, which claimed an estimated sixteen million. **Julie K** can remember it vividly from her childhood. She was only five years old. (That's right—she is one hundred.) It was the year her mother died, and one week later, one of her four-year-old twin brothers followed, both claimed by influenza. In that one year, life expectancy in the United States dropped by twelve years. Julie's father, who lived to be ninety, never remarried.

Living in a motherless home, with an older sister and brothers who were soon at work, Julie soon became responsible for getting the food on the table for the remaining family. Like her neighborhood friends in Poughkeepsie, New York, Julie spoke Italian at home and English at school.

I hated cooking then. It meant I couldn't stay and do any of the things they did after school. I had to go right home. When I had to leave school at fifteen and go to work in a factory—at the sewing machine—I didn't mind because it was what everyone else I knew did.

Julie has always had an excellent memory. She is one of the treasures among us who has not only seen but also remembers the history she has lived—including the dates! She reads newspapers and follows current events regularly. She remembers vividly voting for the first time:

> *You had to be twenty-one. And you had to register. I made a mistake and checked the box for Republican, so when the time came to vote, Republican party workers came to the house to take me to the poll. My father was very upset; I can still hear him yelling in Italian. But I told him not to worry, I voted the right way. When Roosevelt came in in 1932, everything changed. Before that we worked nine hours a day and a half-day on Saturdays, all for eight or nine dollars. After he became president we went to the eight-hour day.*

For the past ten years she has lived with her only son and his partner in an elegant apartment building in center-city Philadelphia.

> *I need to keep busy. I wash and iron for Jim and Rick. And cook. I used to make my own clothes, but now I knit, and I read before I go to sleep. I just finished a book by Anderson Cooper. I stopped driving when I came here. I don't need to in Philly. Everything is nearby or easy to get to. I'm not "overly" religious, but my son goes with me to church every Sunday and on saints' days.*

Nodding toward a large ball of fine mint-green yarn on the coffee table, Julie said it is for a blanket she's working on for a children's hospital in Rhode Island. She recently finished another for their shop; a younger friend volunteers there, and Julie sends them to her to help the fund-raising efforts.

Today Julie, who is petite and beautifully dressed and accessorized, inspires those who know her with her poise, good humor, and sense of completion and peace. She wears a hearing aid and new glasses. She looks back on her own history, her marriage, her widowhood at sixty-two, and her ability to adapt to changes in society and in her own life with a philosophical perspective. Was she shocked or upset when she realized her son was gay?

> *Well, I guess we felt bad about it then, but people can't help what they are. I remember in 1927, my brother was an usher in a wedding. That marriage broke up very quickly. It was annulled. I got the feeling the husband was gay, but no one talked about it then. People shouldn't have to hide.*

What can Julie tell us about reaching the century mark?

> *I never dreamed I'd still be here. I feel good.*

Do you think of this part of life as a gift?

> *Yes. But I'm not a complainer. I believe whatever happens, happens. You can't do much about it. You just go on.*

You seem to be in good spirits.

> *I've always been this way.*

When Julie reflects on key moments in her life, she focuses on times when she realized her strengths. She talks about doing what she had to do and had to face—at five, at fifteen, at twenty-one, as a mother, wife, widow, and now living with her son and his partner. When her husband died suddenly on Cape Cod, she went home to New York City for a month, and her understanding son said, "You know, Mom, I think I ought to take you back to the Cape." She agreed because she recognized the value of the support group—all friends—there. When she got there she assessed her own feelings, consulted friends, bought the mobile home she and her husband had liked, and settled in near the ocean. She loved it and that year sold their co-op in New York City and moved. "If I don't like it, I'll move back to Poughkeepsie where I still have friends," she told her son. Julie realized she was happier where she could always see her next-door neighbors as soon as she stepped outside, instead of in an apartment house.

Recognizing her own needs and the value of friendships and assuming responsibility for her own well-being has been a strong thread in a long life. Even as she has seen the loss of family and contemporaries, Julie has made the best of each situation, made decisions, and allowed herself to enjoy what she can still do. After all, she realizes, not many people celebrate their hundredth birthday with a Caribbean cruise, as she did as the delightful companion of her son and his partner.

NO REGRETS

Wanda R of Nice, California, has an outlook on life that serves her and others well, the "others" being of both the two- and four-footed variety. She has a rule, she says, that works pretty well with all: "I expect the best of people and animals and they usually give it. Sometimes you have to let them know what it is, but when you do, they usually come through." This probably works because Wanda gives her best to them.

At the end of our interview, we asked Wanda what title she would give to a chapter about her life now that she is seventy-three. She thought a minute and said, "I'd call it 'No Regrets.'" Thinking further, she added, "Definitely. I can only think of very minor ones, like placing a cat in the wrong home." How has she reached this point of reflection, self-awareness, self-acceptance, and joy?

"This is the best time of my life!" she said.

Picture one of the most beautiful parts of North America: its largest natural freshwater lake, one of the oldest in North America, stretches before you, with snow-capped mountains in view, and to its south lies the wine region of Napa and Sonoma. Most people there make their living in local businesses or agriculture or in the nearest cities of Ukiah, about thirty miles away, or Santa Rosa, nearly eighty miles away. Wanda lives in Nice (pronounced as in Nice, France), near Clear Lake, California, about a two-hour drive north of San Francisco. She and her ex-husband bought property for rental there in the 1970s while they lived first in San Francisco and then in Mill Valley. Now Bob stays in the Mill Valley house they bought in the late 1960s while Wanda has moved to Clear Lake. Their divorce, after just a few weeks short of forty-nine years of marriage, is friendly enough for each to be comfortable about trading places when either of them finds it convenient (occasionally) to be in the other house.

Obstacles or challenges? Threats or opportunities?

Wanda has always met and tested herself against obstacles, and established her independence since childhood in Northern California. With a mentally ill father, the family moved around the country; Wanda went to four high schools, graduating in Montana before coming back to the Bay area. She waitressed in her teen years, earning the money to attend a two-year college in Marin County and furthering her education with an accounting degree through correspondence courses offered by the University of California. Wanda wanted an office job, and by age twenty, she was working as a bookkeeper/accountant, first for an electrical company and then for a law firm in the financial district.

When one business she worked for closed, Wanda went to the unemployment office and, despite their discouragement, which she found unpleasant, found another job quickly. When it happened again, she decided instead to "reinvent herself." Always an animal lover, she had been helping her mother, who showed Persian cats at cat shows in San Francisco's Cow Palace and other venues.

I decided to start my own business—grooming and breeding Persian cats, which I did for twenty years. I've always loved all animals. When I was young I was into showing and jumping horses, and if I didn't have a bad back, I probably would have wound up shoeing (and showing) horses! When I started breeding cats, I realized that the kitties who weren't going to be show cats were not finding good homes. That's when I met a woman who was rescuing cats. I offered to help since I had a grooming business, and by the year 2000 we became the non-profit Persian and Himalayan Cat Rescue. With its website, www.persiancats.org, PHCR focuses on placing cats of these breeds in Northern California and also throughout the country. I am still involved, on its board and participate in all major decisions.

I will always be involved with animals. I have two big dogs and four cats now at home, all rescue. About five years ago, I went to India with a friend and realized I needed to cut back on my rescue work, which was 24/7. Often I had calls in the middle of the night. I was often taking care of thirty or more cats at a time and was not getting enough sleep. I determined to cut back. My husband was helpful in taking care of the cats while I was away, but when I returned I found out that while I was away he had found "other interests" during the retirement years that he spent up here in Clear Lake managing our property while I was in Mill Valley managing Persian and Himalayan Cat Rescue.

Bob's extramarital interests led to an amicable divorce twenty-one days before their forty-ninth anniversary, after an attempt at reconciliation and recognition of their separate interests and lives. With no children and no malice, dividing their property was less difficult for Wanda and Bob than it might have been and often is for others.

Since moving to Clear Lake, Wanda has been, as always, true to herself, helpful to others, and open to friendships and activities. As a result, she says she couldn't be happier. She understands that she has always needed to be active and has plunged into social activities starting with the Elks (the major social center in town), where she does line dancing and occasionally tends bar, goes on trips and excursions with the Red Hatters, and enjoys a happy relationship with a seventy-six-year-old gentleman she likes and respects. She always has time for new friends and accepts these experiences as ones she might not have appreciated earlier. Wanda doesn't want or expect to marry again; she's happy living on her own. She does plan to attend the wedding in June of an older friend, in her eighties, and says:

> *I understand older people marrying for reasons of finance or health, but that's not for me. Others do it because they don't want to set what they feel would be a bad example for their grandchildren, or other family concerns. But I'm quite content to be on my own and glad to be in a happy relationship. As I said, I have no regrets. Not having children is not a problem: I see people my age having to raise grandchildren or having other problems with children. I'm happy that I know so many wonderful people and have so many good friends. I feel bad when I see people in their fifties and sixties, and I may have been the same, who don't realize that so many people in their seventies, eighties, and nineties are having a ball!*

What are the threads to be found in this chapter that can help us weave joy and optimism into challenging times? Among them, are there any answers to Honey's questions? She asked whether happy and achieving ElderChicks might have laid their plans in advance, or always knew where they were going, or were just lucky, born under the right sign.

One thing is sure: advance planning can be reassuring, even admirable, but it's never a sure thing. The only thing we can count on is change. Yet some characteristics, traits, attitudes appear to serve us particularly well in spite of the changes that are inevitable in life:

- an enduring curiosity about life and other people
- a means of coping with downtimes
- a sense of humor
- the patience to find a new focus for the energy and zest we fear we may be losing
- listening to and learning from others

The women in this chapter are very busy, it's true, but their busyness is of the kind that helps them sleep at night rather than lie awake worrying about what to do with their lives. They are living in the present and remain curious about the future. They approach their lives creatively and find satisfaction interacting with others in positive ways. They focus on what they can do and learn, not what they've lost. And they are willing to make the effort to seek out rewarding activities that will fulfill and reward their days: make the phone calls, find the agencies, commit their time. Is it worth the effort? The women in this chapter believe it is.

You do, too! That's why you're reading this book.

3

I FINALLY HAVE MY FREEDOM AND INDEPENDENCE

How Do I Manage It? How Do I Maintain It?

People often say that this or that person has not yet found himself. But the self is not something one finds; it is something one creates.

—Thomas Szasz

The women in this chapter are experiencing a newly acquired freedom and independence because responsibilities and routines of an earlier stage in their lives have recently changed. A nest emptied of children means a new lifestyle going forward with husband or partner. Divorce or widowhood often requires the assumption of new tasks even as they realize freedom from old ones. Retirement from jobs or careers provides extra free time for activities and interests. We found that some women welcomed their newly acquired freedom and independence but found that they had to guard it closely. Others didn't quite know what to do with it. The women whose stories appear in this chapter tell how they manage to maintain it.

Freedom and independence, we found, are two different issues. Some people that we interviewed felt free but not independent. Some felt independent but not free. We met lots of women who felt fortunate to have both! Let's explore this.

Freedom sounds great, but we all know there is no free lunch. We usually equate freedom with personal liberty, the release from obligations, the power to choose for ourselves limited only by our own needs and wants and the exigencies of nature. When we gain our freedom, we get something, but we give up something in return. For many women, when the nest empties, so does her heart, her purpose, her responsibility to others. When the job becomes history, who is she if no longer defined by her work? Family and career transitions are among the most cataclysmic changes in our lives.

HOW ARE SENIOR WOMEN DEALING WITH THEIR NEW FREEDOM?

As usual, some manage very well, thank you very much. Daily responsibilities to their children are finished when the nest empties. No longer do they have to think about cooking twenty-one meals a week, be sure there's plenty of clean laundry, nag their kids to get those college applications in, worry who the children are driving with. Now time with partners is unscheduled, and they can put their own needs first—without guilt. Some women launched a new career. Some rekindled passions that had long been abandoned for the immediate needs of family care and career. In the generation that preceded us, dreams delayed were most often dreams abandoned forever. This is not true for this generation. Our expectation is for a long life of good quality and limitless possibilities.

Barbara F of Berkeley, California, reported her soon-to-be-emptied-nest experience to us. She recognized that with her children all off to college, newly gained freedom was available to her. She was now free to take her career to a new place. While she had been teaching in schools where the academic calendar mirrored her children's, she now had the time to get an advanced degree, perhaps teach in a college, and pursue her research interests in the field of language development. This was in 1974, which sometimes seems like another era. Maybe she was somewhat ahead of her time in aiming for a career change, but she went for it. She was successful, but the path was not without obstacles to be overcome. Persistence paid off, and today many take for granted what she had to fight for.

> In 1973, I applied to a doctoral program at the University of California at Berkeley. I received, in writing (!), the information that I was welcome to submit an application but should be aware that women of my age (forty-three) are rarely accepted into the program that I wanted to enter. Did I sue the university for unjustly denying me a place because of my age? Of course not. I didn't have the kind of time, money, or the grit it would have taken to go that route, although I had a very supportive husband who was ready to join me in the fight. Besides, I wanted to get on with my career, which until that stage in my life had been secondary to my husband and children. Instead I applied to and successfully completed, in 1980, when I was fifty, a doctoral program at the University of San Francisco. I went on to become a tenured faculty member at Arcadia University, fulfilling all the obligations and responsibilities of academia: publishing, teaching, grant writing, advising, and committee participation. I believe I contributed for another twenty-plus years, in many worthwhile ways, to the university and the students.

Today, what happened to Barbara would not occur, at least not openly. Lots of people set out to advance their careers or develop new ones. No longer are women denied admission because they will "take the place of a man" who won't be slowed by housewifely obligations, pregnancy, motherhood, or the vagaries of menstrual cycles. You may still hear this complaint from some men, but those voices, we hope, are being drowned out and consigned to the fringe. More and more older women are taking charge of their futures, recognize their continuing value to society and themselves, and have large expectations for the rest of their lives. They are taking advantage of their freedom and independence to carve out new places for themselves and weave new dreams. As never before, those dreams are within our reach, if only we are willing to pursue them.

Cheryl L of Newton, Massachusetts, now in her sixties, has broad expectations for her future. Cheryl had a fulfilling career as a lawyer. She is one of the New-Age women who has it all: husband, children, career, friends, hobbies, expectations that life is large and she has much to do. Along the way, however, she realized that her marriage was less satisfying than she felt she had a right to expect. Perhaps her role models—her mother, aunts, and sisters—were willing to live with more limitations than she could tolerate:

> All along, I realized that my relationship with my husband was not as nourishing emotionally as I would have liked or needed. He didn't seem to need anything more than he was getting or giving. But I did. More than anything I wanted my marriage to work for us and our children. I tried everything: talking matters out with him, meditation, couples' therapy, individual therapy, changing my expectations, giving in, making demands, threatening to leave, you name it! Nothing changed the dynamics of our marriage. He was satisfied living in his cocoon with me at his side. I wanted anything but to live in a cocoon.
>
> Then came my decision to retire. My husband's idea of retirement was to play golf and tennis every day, drink cocktails at five, go out to a restaurant, and then settle into an evening of snoozing before the TV screen. He wanted to snooze, and I

wanted to schmooze. I loved my husband, we had made a good life for our family, but this was not the life I wanted for the rest of my life!

I saw myself traveling, volunteering, maybe starting a new business, developing interests I'd put on hold while I was developing my career, reaching out to a world that I needed to explore. He had neither the will nor the energy to join me, although he didn't seem to care what I did with my time as long as I made no demands on his and was there when he needed me.

So how did you handle this dilemma?

The situation became so dire that after thirty-five years of marriage, I filed for divorce. Some of my friends wondered why I didn't just go my own way and he go his but remain married and in the same house. Others wondered why it took me so long to leave.

I left him because I have a great sense of urgency. I'm not ready to pack it in. I see many years—almost a whole 'nother life stretching out ahead of me. I love people, I love adventure, I love to try new ideas, I hope to find a new relationship. Even our sex life was not okay because, frankly, I was feeling like an emotional zero and I wasn't very interested. I missed the affection and better physical sex. I'm looking for much more in life. I know it's out there somewhere for me.

I often wonder whether my mother, aunts, and sisters ever secretly wished for a new chance when they were my age. Could they even have conceived of divorcing a man who is a good economic provider just because he's not a good emotional provider? Would they have considered me selfish to have wanted a life apart from my husband? A life in which I put my own fulfillment first—once my children were grown? Probably not. I do have guilts of my own, or why would I have waited so long? Have I done the right thing? Will I be happy? Have I

damaged him? Have I damaged me? Will my children still love
me? Stay tuned!

Cheryl, after much agonizing, decided that her life was going to
go in a different direction once her newfound freedom kicked in.
She was careful to tell me that she had obsessed for years over her
discontent and that ending the marriage was the most difficult
decision of her life. This seemed like the perfect fork in the road,
with signposts there to be read: if she didn't change direction
now, it would probably never happen. In previous generations,
there might not be such a fork, at least not for most women.
There would have been stigma. There would have been ostra-
cism. There would have been poverty. Cheryl decided to change
her life because many years loom ahead of her, a third of her life
in which to live, learn, and grow.

But other women, unfortunately, are sometimes thrown into a
depression by their newfound, perhaps unsought and unwelcome,
freedom. They experience loss of purpose and loneliness border-
ing on grief. How to fill the void? How to be with their husbands?
How to be brave in the face of change? How to be alone without
being lonely? Many find their freedom oppressive, an albatross.
They know they should be grateful for the release. But they don't
quite know how to manage all that freedom and find themselves
floating aimlessly on a sea of time, aching to be responsible to
someone.

Independence is another matter. Independence means not being
controlled by others, thinking for oneself. Independent people
take care of themselves. This requires confidence and compe-
tence. In our generation, as in our mothers,' many women do not
bother their pretty little heads with financial matters such as bro-
kerage accounts and income tax or the purchase of "masculine"
items such as cars, insurance, and mortgages. Repairing broken

household things is usually reserved for the *honeydew* list, as in, "Honey, do fix the light in the bathroom, please." Nothing is wrong with this division of roles—if both parties agree to the arrangement. But what happens when a spouse divorces, dies, or becomes physically incapacitated and unable to maintain the role that worked so well in the past? This can be a real game changer.

Blanche Burton-Lyles of Philadelphia, Pennsylvania, who will tell her story in chapter 10, also believes that freedom and independence are not quite the same thing. Freedom, she feels, is a state of mind.

> *It's about how and what I think. It belongs to me and to me alone. Independence is something else. I may cherish it, but I might not be able to choose it. For many people it means realizing that you may need to depend on others for some things as you get older. I may be powerless to maintain my independence, but I am free to cope as I wish.*

Sandy L of Cherry Hill, New Jersey, looks back at eighty and realizes that things have worked out a lot better than she might have expected:

> *My mother often quoted the old saying, "Comparisons are odious." She tried to impress on me that it's not a good thing to compare what you have or do to what the next person has or is doing. But now that I find myself at this age still married to Jerry, who is eighty-three, I realize that life is good in many ways that I didn't consciously think about when I was younger. Was it good fortune? Instinct? The fact that he was unthreatened by my own dreams or opportunities?*
>
> *I've always had my own dreams and ideas, and when I was able, I followed them. When he wasn't particularly interested, I understood and didn't expect him to embrace them. If my work or interests took me away from home, he understood that we remained a solid unit but able to act on our own respon-*

sibly. I think younger women of today are more likely to main-
tain a sense of independence within marriage or partnerships
than many of my acquaintances were because they have a
stronger sense of who they are as individuals. At least I hope
so.

I recognize that looming health issues may make more and
more demands on each of us, but I'm hopeful that past experi-
ence of mutual respect will inform decisions that probably lie
ahead. We hope to remain able to maintain our awareness of
each other's independent and mutual needs.

Blanche's observation that "freedom is a state of mind" has been
evident to **Jean A**, now of Philadelphia, Pennsylvania, since her
youth, and she's never lost that sense of freedom, although life's
circumstances may have seriously compromised her ability to be
independent at earlier stages. When Jean was ten years old she
discovered the life and writings of Roy Chapman Andrews, the
famous explorer, naturalist, and writer who became the director
of the American Museum of Natural History. When she read of
his extraordinary adventures and discoveries in Asia, a great curiosity was born. Jean did not actually fulfill her childhood dream of
seeing Mongolia until she finally did cross the Gobi Desert some
seventy years later. But cross it she did, despite all the intervening
years and the considerable trials they brought. She says, "I'll go
anywhere I can read the signs—and some where I can't."

We learned about Jean's early life:

Jean was born in Toledo, Ohio, grew up in Chicago, and arrived in Philadelphia in the 1940s with a scholarship to the University of Pennsylvania, where she channeled her considerable
energy into running student government and becoming valedicto-
rian. She immersed herself in studying archaeology and anthropology and, as part of the US Archaeological Field School and

during her graduate studies, excavated in Arizona, France, and South Florida.

As was true for so many women, marriage and family created situations of interdependency: a husband's needs as a graduate student in the same field, a daughter's birth, and the needs of a seventeen-month-old son precluded their travel to India on his Fulbright award. In addition, her children developed special needs—her daughter's vision impairment and her son's epilepsy as a result of encephalitis precipitated by measles. Fortunately, Jean and her husband were able to stay in the United States on a joint Ford Foundation fellowship to study colloquial Mongolian.

Both the need to form realistic expectations and practicality led her to earn a degree in library science, and Jean was able eventually to work for twenty-five years as the librarian for the University of Pennsylvania's renowned Museum of Archaeology and Anthropology. As someone knowledgeable in the field who revels in the "sleuthing," as she says, "of research and digging, both in dirt and documents," Jean was thus prepared for the kind of independence brought on when her husband left her. "Aren't men funny?" says Jean. "He married another very small woman with short, blond, curly hair—and a librarian!" While Jean had a loving relationship with a wonderful man who has since died, she has always preferred living on her own since her divorce.

> I've lived in my small house on a little street in an old, colonial part of Philadelphia for thirty-six years. People know and help one another here. I know that in an emergency, I could call any of five people to get me to the hospital. If I ever need to, I would prefer putting a small stairlift in my narrow staircase to moving out. I love my neighbors and have loved watching their kids grow up. Recently, I gave my wedding dress to the young woman across the street.

Jean, her daughter, and her son-in-law enjoy a loving relationship respectful of each other's independence. She continues to fulfill her lifelong dream of travel and study. When she finally felt she was able to go to Mongolia at last (at age seventy-nine), she found a Lutheran choirmaster's group from California who would be there for the festivals she had known about for so many years and went with them.

> *It was worth the two days' travel and the day to sleep it off to be there for two weeks. I even startled the guides and myself when I was able to translate some of the signs. When I actually got to where the dinosaur skeletons were found, I had to "go." Of course, that meant "going" behind the tent. One of the young guides said, "Well, you got to mark your spot on the Flaming Cliffs of Mongolia." I was thrilled.*

Among the many pictures, notes, and sayings on her refrigerator, Jean has a permanent one by the Chinese philosopher Lao-Tze in the Tao Te Ching: "A person with outward courage dares to die; a person with inner courage dares to live."

From where does this strong need for independence among some people spring? For some it seems to be present in childhood and never stops influencing their decisions. **Jeanne L**, who wants her identity withheld, is a case in point. Jeanne now runs a thriving business, a second career that she started when she retired from her job. Here is her story:

> *From the vantage point today of my seventy-eight years I am still amazed that at seventeen years of age I had the strength to leave home. My father had been sexually abusing me. My mother, though a devout Christian, denied that this was going on. I knew then that I would either be spending the rest of my life in an institution or have to get on with my life so I could put all this horror behind me. I decided that leaving home was my only salvation. I managed to convince my grandmother to lend me money to go to nursing school. And so at seventeen, I left home and saved my life. It has been a good one and I have*

never regretted my choice. I have remained devoted to my Christian faith and know that it is my faith that has sustained me throughout life.

Jeanne started off as an independent youngster and treasures her independence to this day. It seems that nothing can quash her strength and purpose.

JoAnne K of Chicago, Illinois, found herself suddenly plunged into a situation of unwelcome independence. Her life had been tranquil and pleasant, and she felt she had safely placed herself in her husband's hands: being a wife and a mother of three, playing tennis, gardening, and taking part in book groups took up much of her time. But slowly, she began to have suspicions that her husband of twenty-five years was becoming less attentive to her.

He began to criticize my hair, my makeup, whatever I wore. He was always the life of every party and I wasn't, so I figured he was getting bored with me. I started to tell jokes and stories, but they usually fell flat. I realized I was trying to compete with him but I couldn't do it well. I even had a face-lift to try to improve my looks. Then one day, my life fell apart. He announced that he had fallen in love with his young office assistant. He claimed he loved us both and really was beside himself with pain and guilt—but not enough to give her up.

We went through a year of roller-coasting emotions, therapy, and "now-I'll-see-her-now-I-won't" promises. Our kids were off at college. They weren't dealing with my everyday misery. I don't want to go through all the awful details. Let's just say that finally the marriage ended.

I was devastated. There were many sleepless nights, too much alcohol, lots of crying, lots of antidepressants, even thoughts of suicide. I felt so rejected and so much a failure. I couldn't manage my finances or make decisions about things that cost a great deal of money. I realized I had absolutely no confidence in myself about certain things.

Was there a turning point?

Thank God I had two hands, because on the other hand, I had some really good friends, I went to a really good support group, saw a wonderful therapist, and found that my children, who loved their father but were pretty mad at him, were very supportive of me.

I finally took myself in hand. I faced the fact that he didn't love me anymore and the marriage was never going to be patched together. But the real turning point came when I realized that he was the bad guy here, not me. And then I didn't want him back!

I went back to school for a master's degree in psychology and became thoroughly immersed in it. The courses focused on self-understanding and self-reflection. Somehow, I saw that looking inward held an answer for me. I began to realize that all my married life I had tried to change myself into what I thought he wanted me to be. How wrong that was! Instead, I set out to find out who I am, and I think I was successful. I also realized that those decisions I didn't think I was capable of making weren't so hard after all. Bargaining with a car dealer? Balancing the checkbook? Figuring out which insurance company is best? Big deal! None of that is so hard, just an extra burden.

Eventually I opened a private psychology practice in an office with a few other part-time therapists. This became the center of my life. I still play tennis and take care of my garden, am a mother to my grown children, am learning to play bridge, and go to my book group. I also go out on dates, but I'm not in a hurry to tie myself down to a husband or partner. Once burned, twice careful? Maybe. I know I'll consider it if the right guy comes along. But I finally have a career that I love.

*I'm not by nature a Pollyanna, but I do know that I am a much
stronger person now than I was before all this happened.*

JoAnne's is a steep price to pay for learning who you are and how
to manage your life. But learn it she did. She was finally freed
from her *perceived* idea of marriage—pleasing her husband at the
expense of herself. JoAnne went on to say that if she marries or
partners again, it will be on different terms, because now she
knows who she is.

Prizing their freedom and independence was a motif we heard
over and over from women of all ages and backgrounds. But not
uncommon were a group of women who found that their families
really didn't respect their strong need to remain independent.
Maintaining independence when family members doubt your
ability to handle it was a recurring theme and an issue fraught
with stress. Some battled with children urging them to move
across the country to be close to *them* (but far away from their
own friends and satisfying lives) or into "retirement" situations
before they were ready to do so. Is this for the comfort and
benefit of the children or of the parents? Recognizing when or if
you need to be dependent on others, even if it means giving up
where you live, is one of the major issues facing seniors.

Here is how other women we interviewed coped with their
experiences of freedom and independence:

Martha G of Sarasota, Florida, reported this in a whisper. She
wanted no one to hear what she told me. She confessed that if I
had been someone she would ever see again, she never would tell
me this. Of course, she requested anonymity.

*I kind of feel a little guilty sometimes. I had a great marriage
and I loved my husband dearly. Marriage is a series of ongoing*

compromises, and we both got a lot in return for striking those spoken and unspoken bargains. But now that I'm alone, I can do whatever I want, when, how, and with whom. It's a big price to pay, and I would not have chosen this. But it is a compensation, and I do enjoy that freedom. I don't know if I could ever give it up. And you know what else? I'm glad I don't have to deal with all that sex business. It was all right when we were younger, but I don't want it at all now, and I don't have to feel guilty about it, like I did when he was alive. That's a kind of freedom too.

Linda E of Brookline, Massachusetts, carried that thought further and had this to say:

Seven years ago I was widowed when I was sixty-three. What a shock! No illness, no warning. It happened in an automobile accident with a drunk driver. It took me a long time to get over my grief and move on. My husband and children had been the center of my life and I loved them all dearly. We had made a beautiful home together, and we were a great support to each other when this tragedy occurred. Now my husband was gone and the children were out of my nest and in nests of their own.

Friends urged me into the marriage path. "You have many years left to create a new relationship as good as the one you lost," they said. "Meet this guy, date that guy, this one would be such a good catch, that one's loaded and you'll never have to worry about money again, there's no reason to stay single." No reason? I found plenty of reasons!

A strange thing was happening to me as I moved forward with my life. I have always really liked to be with people, men as well as women—and I still do. I run a small public relations consulting business and also lead a very active social life. I go to movies, plays, concerts, political meetings, lectures, good restaurants, and almost always am accompanied by friends. But I very much enjoy my own company and prefer it to being with someone I don't particularly like. My friends want to "fix me up" on dates, but what I sense from a lot of the men I meet is that they, often recently single themselves, are in real need of someone to take care of their meals, their socks, and their social calendars. I'm not willing to take on that role again.

So who are you now?

Well, another thing I learned about myself once the pain of my grief began to dissipate is that I really, really like my freedom. I realize that I am finished with marriage compromises. Sometimes I just want to put up my feet and not talk to anyone when I walk in my house after a full day of whatever. Sometimes I don't want to give up what I want to do to accommodate to someone else's wishes. I don't want to make my house compatible with someone else's tastes. I just want to please my own.

I want to spend my retirement in my own way. I want to continue to feel free to invite someone in for a weekend, or a week, or to take a trip together. I enjoy sex when I have it and miss it when it's missing. But I don't want someone moving in with me on a permanent basis. I like separate but equal when it comes to my relationships with adults. I don't feel I need or want to make a commitment to marriage or a partner now. Happily, my kids understand that this attitude works for me at this time in my life, and they are comfortable with it.

Sound selfish? Maybe so. On the other hand, I have spent my entire married life putting the needs of my family ahead of mine. Maybe the time is right for me to become a confirmed bachelor. After all, why should that loaded term be available for men only?

Linda is a strong woman who manages her independence well and is not afraid to wear her freedom as a crown. We found that not wanting to remarry is not unique among the women we met, although few would actually admit that this new freedom has become a source of happiness for them. More women than not seemed to feel guilty about enjoying a freedom that had been gained as a result of their husband's death or even admitting that there can be an upside to widowhood.

Esther R of Monroe Township, New Jersey, a delightful woman in her mid-seventies, obviously cherishing her freedom and independence, modestly says she's not involved in any kinds of constructive projects. Her clear-eyed assessment of her own life and her place in the lives of her family and friends, her sense of humor, and her appreciation of the positive aspects of her life make her a person loved and appreciated by the people she knows. We disagree that she "doesn't do anything constructive." Nurturing her many relationships with others is truly a constructive project! She brings much happiness and spirit into many lives. We love people who savor their freedom and enrich the lives of others. Here's what Esther told us:

> *I don't know what my husband would be like in retirement. Unfortunately, he didn't live to retirement age. I never earned a lot of money, so that doesn't define the difference between my working days and my retirement. Whatever I did always involved people, and that remains my main activity in retirement: being with friends, entertaining, volunteering. I'm not involved in any kinds of constructive projects. I feel no guilt. In fact, when I have a disturbed night's sleep, I'm glad I don't have to go to work. I think, "Well, I can go back to sleep or take a nap." I'm very happy being retired, and I've been retired for a long time—since I was sixty-two.*

Roslyn B of Philadelphia, Pennsylvania, and her husband, Marvin, were happily winding down successful careers and ramping up successful retirements when an accident intervened. In a flash their long-awaited independence and their precious freedom were lost. For quite a while after this blow to their lives, Roz and Marvin felt overwhelmed and worried about their ability to cope with all the health problems that suddenly consumed their lives.

Marvin was confined to a wheelchair and needed almost twenty-four-hour health care. They lived in a three-story house crammed with a lifetime of possessions. The whole burden of care was on Roz's shoulders. And she understood that a positive attitude is at the heart of the healing process. How many angels can there be within us?

However, with spunk and grit, Roz found the resources she wasn't certain she had. She reads a book a day and goes to movies and plays alone rather than abandon her interests. Her ability to form and maintain close relationships keeps her in touch with and involved in the world beyond her husband's wheelchair. She has learned that independence has many definitions, and she has found the ones that work for her.

Change which occurs because of monumental accidents happens before we realize the occasion or consequences. My husband and I were two young old folks enjoying our golden years when we collided with a speeding car. My husband of fifty-two years suffered a broken neck, reducing his mobility to life in a wheelchair.

He is astonishing in his remaining vitality and interest in family and friends, but his frustrations and difficulties have robbed us of our former lives. As a consequence of being his major caregiver, I have felt as if I had little to say to you ElderChicks: I haven't felt any mastery of our senior life. My independence and freedom? Gone! Our lives from now on would revolve around medical appointments and handicap ramps.

As the reality of our new circumstances became clear, I realized I must sell the large house stocked with my husband's lifelong collections of everything imaginable and buy a condo so we could live on one floor. Daily decisions and immediate judgments were in my hands alone. Maybe I would make irrevocable mistakes—we had always made the big choices together.

Recently, however, I realized my error. I am seventy-nine years old, in good health, have two unexpected and delightful grandchildren, two lovely daughters whose careers are genuinely contributing to the betterment of society, and the aid of an astonishing young man from Libya (my husband's caregiver) who has become a son, beloved by all of us. With the help of friends, we get out a bit. My most available regular source of personal indulgence is reading. I read almost a book a day, escaping my worries with mysteries, crime fiction, adventure, and biography. When necessary, I made the big decisions on my own, and I have become stronger for them. Although in some ways I gave up independence, in other ways I gained.

I'd very much like to be doing something more with my life but as yet have been unable to find the time or capability. But I'm working on it, and I do believe I'm finding my way.

Roslyn is hardly independent. She is completely tied to the physical situation that confines both her and her husband. Yet she has managed to find a way to free herself, sometimes if not always, from the dependency of her husband on her. It became apparent during the rest of the afternoon that Roz takes great joy in the good fortune of others. She remains in close touch with her friends, sharing equally in the good or bad that befalls them. Though no longer independent, she feels she has the freedom to flee with her mind from the constant obligation and constraints of her husband's disabled life.

Unlike Roslyn, who found her husband unexpectedly and forever dependent on her, **Marylen Oberman** of Ann Arbor, Michigan, suddenly, at age fifty-eight, found herself, while in the midst of a busy and rewarding career, dependent on everyone else—and it nearly was her undoing. She told us the grim story of her accident and recovery.

I had heard the loud collision but hadn't seen it. With me on its grille, the car smashed into the store's brick wall and set off a burglar alarm. Suddenly, everything stopped. I lay on my back, nine hundred miles from home, crushed between the sidewalk and the inside of a store window, until the ambulance took me away.

And that started my eighteen-month uphill climb to recovery. As each day passed and I was still in the hospital, I began to notice changes in me. I was no longer the upbeat woman working at a career that I loved. (Me, retire? No way!) But in the blink of an eye, life had beaten me down. Most of the time, I was frustrated and disappointed and wondered what was to become of me. I found that lying in bed day after day—without much movement or much progress either—had made me passive and dependent. It had cooled my fire. I had to cope constantly with bone grafts, skin grafts, hyperbaric chambers, external fixators, metal stabilizers, and the twenty-seven operations that were necessary to mend my crushed bones. And pain! More pain than my body or soul could endure.

You don't look beaten down to me, Marylen. How have you coped?

"Face it, Marylen! You're at a crossroads in your life." I actually started to talk to myself, give myself pep talks. I knew it would be easy to just give in and feel sorry for myself. But I realized that I could apply all my years of helping others regain strength to myself. I knew that if I put all my energy into healing, I would have the strength to see the brighter side of each day. I knew that people would gather around me to support me as I tried to conquer each day, one at a time.

Don't think I was a model of sunny disposition. And don't think I would have been able to reach recovery alone. My health-care providers were a cross between angel and healer, performing daily, unpleasant, menial tasks for this sick, often cranky person. The doctors, aides, friends, my husband (who was my best friend), and our children were the coaches and cheerleaders who coaxed me back to health, hope, and vitality.

It's fifteen years later, and I still need weekly physical therapy, orthotics in my specially made shoes, and a daily exercise regimen in order to enjoy my wonderful life, which I now know is very, very fragile. A person's life has its own agenda with ups, downs, and challenges. No one asks to be in a car accident. No one asks for cancer. We may find ourselves in bad straits, disoriented, and not prepared to cope. But we have no choice, really, except to make peace with whatever happens. So we educate ourselves, stay grounded, and do the best we can with the situations we can control. Throughout the years I have made many choices that were within my control. Some were easy, some difficult, and some plain impossible, but they were mine to decide. Acceptance and adjustment to situations beyond my control are my greatest ongoing challenges. What I have learned is that it pays off to spend all my energy on the things I can affect and not to waste my time and energy on the things I cannot. But it's not always easy to know the difference."

Fortunately, Marylen gritted her teeth, gathered her strength, and chose the hard, uphill path. "I *will* not give up my independence" became her mantra. She marshaled her resources and carried on. What inner strengths she called upon! Marylen copes with adversity in a characteristic manner. She

- first complains to acknowledge reality

- always searches for silver linings

- accepts the help of friends (when she's not giving them help)

- channels her anger toward herself when her resolve flags

- keeps her situation in sensible perspective

- maintains interest and involvement in the world

As serious and traumatic as her problems and solutions were—and still are—Marylen avoids self-involvement, finding much about herself to laugh at and much about the needs of others to care for. She also found strength in writing a book about her ordeal.[1] Marylen also went on to use what she learned from her long battle with serious physical challenges to develop and teach courses in what she calls "journal writing for healing."

WHERE TO LIVE . . . HOW TO LIVE

Looking toward retirement or suddenly finding themselves smack in its middle has spurred the interest of burgeoning numbers of Boomers and seniors. Some of the language is changing, too. We hear about living "intentionally" or being "deterministic about the future" in relation to whether to enter a new kind of community or "to age in place." **Lynne Iser** at sixty-two looks ahead both intentionally and with determination. She has founded the Center for Growing Older in Community in Philadelphia. Lynne spoke over coffee in the sunny breakfast room of her house in West Mount Airy, an old section of Philadelphia known for its ethnic diversity and vibrant attention to new ideas.

> *I realize that for the most part, we cannot control when life ends, but we can make some decisions about how we spend the time until then. Beginning to recognize mortality gave me a little kick in the pants, but I'm happy I got here. When I think about what I want to leave behind, the question arises: "How will I do whatever that is?" I may remember the dream of being a dancer and realize I've danced enough. We all have dreams. I didn't take that road; how do I do my road? In reviewing our lives, we need to give up the things we may resent, the things that make us unhappy, forgive ourselves for what we've done or didn't do.*

When Lynne was a single mother with a master's degree in public
health, she was the founding executive director of the Spiritual
Eldering Institute[2] in Boulder, Colorado. There for ten years, she
developed the foundation of the philosophy and principles she
lives by, striving to empower people in the second half of life to
develop their resources and wisdom to create a world that is sus-
tainable, just, and fulfilling. Now married and with a blended
family, she says:

> *What we can do now is recontextualize our life—put a new
> perspective on it. And in order to do this psychospiritual/ag-
> ing-well work effectively, I believe we need to do it in commu-
> nity. The idea of salons for conversation, being less alone,
> creating interdependence with your neighbors on physical,
> emotional, and spiritual levels led to my interest in cohousing.
> I became interested in the movement for senior cohousing
> based on a Danish model, where it already exists.*

Finding resources also in the work of architect Charles Durrett,[3]
Lynne is gathering a cadre of like-minded people who have identified a space within the city, and therefore accessible to its amen-
ities, to build the houses they will occupy. Interaction will be
facilitated by the physical plan: kitchens facing pedestrian walk-
ways, common spaces for meetings and planned events, a mailbox
center and spaces for visiting children. Lynne is encouraged in
her work by her observation that there are now about one hundred such communities across the country, ranging from those
which include young families to those for senior participants ex-
clusively. What she continues to learn and how she continues to
grow spiritually, emotionally, and intellectually sustains her.

DIFFERENT STROKES FOR DIFFERENT FOLKS

Living in community is not for everyone. **Suzanne R** of Boston, Massachusetts, is seventy-five and determined to remain in the city home she loves and lived in with her husband until his death three years ago. Then she heard about the Aging in Place movement and decided to join the village.

> *I love Boston, and I'm fortunate to live in a city with so much to do. I belong to Beacon Hill Village, which I think is providing a model for other cities that have seniors who want to "age in place," the current term for staying in one's own home. When my husband was alive, we organized our own activities easily, with and without other people. I found it harder to do things alone and, let's face it, I wasn't always as comfortable with other couples after he died. The "village" is not a village of homes; it's an organization that arranges a broad spectrum of activities which village members can attend. The yearly membership fee for this service is fairly expensive for me, but I find it's worth it because so many events and services are included—and I never need to go alone.*
>
> *I am much more likely to attend a movie, lecture, or museum with a group than alone. Being part of the village is making it much easier to maintain my independence. They even help me find the people I need when something goes wrong in the house or I need help or advice about health matters. I've even made new friends on group walks around the city and excursions to places I'd rather not drive to anymore, especially alone.*

Joan and her husband, **Arthur**, of Palo Alto, California, decided, in their youthful and vigorous early eighties, that "rattling around" in their large house just emphasized the loneliness they felt in a neighborhood now populated with younger families that didn't know them very well.

We hesitate to go out at night sometimes because it means coming home late at night to a garage that could hide an un-welcome "visitor." Our fears were actually restricting our inde-pendence and freedom to do what we want. Many of our friends have moved to various retirement living situations, and we began to realize that those people seem to have more free-dom and independence than we have. My husband hated that he would have to put on a jacket for dinner and eat in a group dining hall every night at whatever hour they said we had to eat. But we weighed all the pros and cons and decided that at our age, this would be a good thing, and it is. There are lots of activities, but we only do what interests us. We don't always eat in the dining room, and when we come home at night we feel safe. In many ways our freedom and independence have been expanded rather than restricted. We are very happy here.

SHOULD I STAY WHERE I AM? SHOULD I GO WHERE MY KIDS LIVE? HOW WILL THIS AFFECT MY INDEPENDENCE?

Sometimes adult children try to interfere with their parents' free-dom and independence by wanting their parents to do what is easiest for them. This was the complaint of **Sally** and **Steve S** of Milwaukee, Wisconsin. They have recently retired from their jobs and are looking forward to travel, leisure, starting some new hob-bies, and getting to know their grandchildren who live far away. Sally is in her late sixties. She is a breast cancer survivor, and her husband is recovering well from recent heart bypass surgery. They are both healthy enough to be playing tennis again as well as working out. They lead active lives: he's a consultant in his field of hospital administration; she's involved in various volunteer activ-ities. They have decided that their three-story home is more than they need or want at this time in their lives, and they are now actively condo hunting. Their three children and families live in other cities a plane ride away.

Enter the children, who now weigh in on the decision. Sally is wishing they would get uninvolved.

Our children are concerned that if we get ill again, they will have to come in from where they live to care for us. Why, they ask, can't we buy or rent a condo in one of their cities so we would be close to at least one of our children? Then they wouldn't have to worry about us. They feel we would be closer to the grandchildren and more a part of their lives. They love us very much and want to be sure we are safe, secure, and get the best of care, which they feel they can provide for us. It feels to us that they don't trust our judgment to make good decisions about ourselves. Since when did we become so incompetent? After all, we raised them to be good, strong, capable adults, didn't we? And since when did our needs become less important than theirs?

I can sort of see their point. Do you view this as a hardship?

We don't want to move to a new city at this time in our lives. Our friends are here, we love Milwaukee, we can manage the weather, our activities are set, we know the way, and I like my hairdresser. But what I like least about this whole thing is that our children are turning us into their children, and they are acting like our parents. We resent being infantilized. Now that we've reached a period of freedom from a lot of the responsibility of raising our children, we are loving the idea that we're free to make decisions based on our needs and desires.

The problem is I know they believe they are doing what is best for us. And maybe they're right. We do want the family to remain a close unit. Perhaps it can't if we live so far apart. And we do have major illnesses which may cause havoc in our lives in the near future. Do we take a chance and wait until the boom lowers on us (move to Portland later, when we get sick)? Or do we act with prudence and prepare for the worst (move to Portland now and wait there to get sick)? We find all this depressing and can't decide what to do! I don't like this on-the-

one-hand-but-on-the-other-hand kind of decision. With a little
bit of luck, we have a whole third of our lives left. We could be
living somewhere we don't want to live for a long time. Bum-
mer!

Adele C of Collingswood, New Jersey, has almost two decades on
Sally but is facing the same dilemma. Her children also want to
influence where she lives. She, too, leads an active and vital life.
Adele still works as a travel agent. She has been weighing the pros
and cons of moving from New Jersey to Florida. She finds the
weather more forgiving than the harsh northern winters. Her son
lives nearby with his family, whom she loves and sees regularly.

As a financial planner, my son finds me a challenge, but as I
tell him, I own my house, I own my car, and I still earn a living
from my travel business and get the benefit of continuing to
travel. I love being with him, his wife, and my grandson. I go
there for dinner every other Sunday—that's six hours a month.
Is six hours a month reason to stay? I know I could create a
support system in Florida. I know people there and would
move to a retirement community.

My daughter-in-law, who has a very responsible job, says, "We
can't be flying down to Florida when you get sick." True, I've
survived cancer three times, including two mastectomies and
the loss of one lung, but I've never let that stop me; I can cope
with needing new doctors there and whatever happens.

I also see that when my daughter-in-law's parents come from
England to visit, they stay two weeks, and she and my son
always show them a lovely time. I think I'll do better having
them visit me in Florida than I do here. And with the kind of
travel planning work I do, I can work there just as well. All I
need is a telephone and a laptop. If I can sell my house profit-
ably, I think I will go.

HOW TO SEE CLEARLY NOW

Below is a template for solving a great variety of problems, including Sally's, Steve's, and Adele's. Creating and filling in a table or a chart is a good way to clarify the issues.

1. First, state the problem clearly. Many problems—not just this one—can be clarified using this method.

2. Then start writing. It is important to write down your thoughts and their thoughts—*in complete sentences!* That way, you can see the logic (or illogic) of both sets of arguments. (Remember your school days: complete sentences express complete ideas; a half-sentence expresses only half an idea.)

As an example, we have chosen a problem that increasingly affects seniors, given the mobility of our society today. We know many people who have picked up roots because of their own and their children's fears about aging and poor health. And the result is not always happy. The move is often mired in a confusion of the emotional costs and dividends. Take a look at this table as a way of sorting through your thoughts. **Be sure to ask your children to do the same.**

You get the idea.

Table 3.1.   How to Clarify Your Thoughts.

Problem: Our daughter wants us to move to the city she lives in because we are getting older and she doesn't think we should be alone. We're not sure we want to do that.

Their Thoughts	Our Thoughts	What Can Be Done
1. You live so far away. What happens if one of you gets sick or frail?	1. Good point! That worries us, too.	1a) Prepare! Get long-term care insurance. 1b) Find a local retirement community where you'll be cared for *and* near your friends.
2. It would be so nice if you could live closer to your grandchildren. And we would love to see more of you.	2. But we'll be leaving all our friends and activities behind. It's not so easy to make new connections at our age.	2. We'll learn to Skype, text, tweet, and do Facebook. We'll keep up with modern technology *and* our grandchildren. It's good for the mind. We'll visit at times convenient for our children and grandchildren.
3. We both work and have children to care for. We can't come to where you live whenever you might need us. Who would oversee the health-care providers?	3. Another good point! We're worried about that, too.	3a) Prepare! Get long-term care insurance. 3b) That's what retirement communities are for. 3c) Make arrangements with friends to keep an eye on each other's needs.
4. It's time for you to get rid of that big house and all those things!	4a) We love those "things"—they're a lifetime of memories. 4b) I'd like a lesser house and less responsibility. How do I get my husband to move to a condo much less to another city? 4c) Can I afford the move?	4a) Okay, we can get rid of a lot of the stuff. Here's where *you* can help. 4b) See chapter 2. We'll move to a condo. Much more manageable and there's a ready-made community close at hand. 4c) Discuss this with the appropriate professionals. Don't make unchecked guesses.

4

WE LOVE OUR POSSESSIONS BUT THEY ARE STARTING TO OWN US

How Do I Downsize My Life?

*I like to walk about amidst
the beautiful things that adorn the world;
but private wealth I should decline,
or any sort of personal possessions,
because they would take away my liberty.*
—George Santayana

LET'S GET ONE THING CLEAR. IT'S NOT ABOUT THE THINGS

It's about change. It's about letting go. It's about who we are without our lifetime of possessions. It's about whether getting rid of the mementos diminishes all that we have experienced. In our conversations with many women, this was one of the most recurrent concerns. They know it's time to live smaller, shed stuff, move on. *But*:

- Inertia takes over.

- Men dig in their feet.

- Women faint on their fainting couches.

- Grown children wonder what's to become of their childhood.

Everyone knows it is an issue that has to be faced, and sooner is better than later.

SMALLER HOUSE, LARGER LIFE

Elena S took the bull by the horns and decided that the time to downsize is now.

> *I am no longer owned by my stuff. A long time ago, I realized that one of the reasons I loved traveling was that I had very few things with me—fewer clothes, shoes, make-up, and so on. I liked the freedom that I felt having to look after fewer things.*

And **Barbara F** told us this:

> *When I got back from vacation one year our house didn't look as good to me as it used to. The walls needed painting, the furniture looked tired, there was too much stuff, and I didn't feel like (and really couldn't afford) the hassle of a makeover. Much as I loved my home, I felt shackled by it in a way. It always demanded something: fresh paint, roof repair, a plumbing fix. I envied my friends in condos who could pick themselves up at a moment's notice and leave—for a weekend, a month, a year. All they had to do was stop the newspapers and hold the mail. I longed for that freedom. It was like a ticket to another life.*
>
> *Our kids had left home, many of our neighbors had moved to condos, and the new neighbors looked on us as some kind of relic. They were not really our friends, although most of them—the ones who even knew we were here—were very nice*

to us. Besides, I didn't know where to start sorting through this accumulation of a lifetime. The very thought of it gave me a headache! Every time I suggested to my husband that maybe it's time to move, he scowled into his newspaper and told me how happy he is in our house. I knew we were not getting any younger and the time would come when this house might be too much for us to manage. And suppose something "happened" to one of us. Then the other of us would be facing two bad choices—alone:

- *the loneliness and vulnerability of living in this huge old house alone*

- *breaking up our home and selling this huge old house—also alone*

Equally bad choices! Uh-oh! Here comes another sleepless night because I know the time is now!

As we traveled around the country interviewing women individually, during our Lunch and Listens, and at the workshops we presented, this issue never failed to come up. Whether it was a move to smaller quarters or another city or just feeling smothered by having too much stuff around, downsizing is very much on the minds of sixty-plus women. Some don't want to think about it, but it nags at them anyway; others meet it head on. We found that these questions must be answered before any decision can be made:

- *Why* is this move a good idea?

- *Where* should we go?

- *When* should this move take place?

- *What* should we keep?

- *Who* gets the stuff we give away?

- *How* do we dispose of our things?

WHY IS THIS MOVE A GOOD IDEA? WHERE SHOULD WE GO?

Hannah H and her husband were in their eighties when they checked out the blueprints of a retirement community in Sarasota, Florida, under construction among lots of trees, wetlands, pools, and gardens—and they allowed dogs. Even at their age, they had the spirit and courage to recognize that a change in lifestyle would be worth the effort. The increased services were the *why*, observing new construction in their neighborhood was the *where*, and they knew that now was the *when*. Here is what Hannah told us:

> *My husband and I had been comfortably living in a villa in a golf course community in southwestern Florida—he in his early nineties and I in my early eighties and our two-year-old poodle. We had no thoughts of living elsewhere until I saw, while driving around in our neighborhood, a senior facility under construction. Well, it did not take long to convince my husband that now was the time to make the move to another style of living—and we did.*
>
> *My husband truly enjoyed the two and a half years we've lived here. Since his death, I realize it was one of the best decisions we had made. With the conveniences of services, food, and companionship available for me, I was/am able to continue my community activities while enjoying the comforts of home.*
>
> *If I were to advise others it would be to think ahead, plan ahead, and accept change positively.*

HOW DO I TACKLE THE CONTENTS OF A LARGE HOUSE?

Barbara F dealt with the problem in this way:

Unloading the accumulation of things from a long and busy marriage seemed like something to avoid at all cost. However, I finally bit the bullet and made a plan. In our big house I had a big basement. I had long ago learned that once the children leave the nest, the house they grew up in remains terribly important because it becomes the place where they store their stuff. Dismantling the home also may have symbolized something like the final giving up of their childhood. My children live in England, California, and Massachusetts.

So I sat on the floor in the basement and got on the phone. I went through all their things one by one—with them at the other end of the line—and told them I was shipping all their things to them this week. Was there anything they could bear to part with? You'd be amazed at how little they wanted when they heard that as of next week their stuff had to fit into their closets. This process thinned out the clutter considerably.

The second task was to decide what to do with the rest. I divided the basement of our home into four quarters. In one part I put the things I planned to give to a foundation which could use the furniture. I called them before I could change my mind, and they were happy to receive it. They brought a van and took it away, and we took a tax deduction. In the second quarter, I put a few items I hoped to, and actually did, sell. The third quarter contained a pile of things for donation to Goodwill. They sent a truck to pick up that stuff, too. The fourth quarter contained things I wanted to take to the new condo that had been stored in the basement. I'm ashamed to say that a few of those boxes had been stored intact from a previous move, and to this day they haven't been unpacked! I'm not even sure what they contain under the mysterious label Mementos.

It sounds as though you are a pretty organized person. Everyone tells us how hard it is to go from big to small.

It is! You just have to set the alarm and get down to work. Once you actually start, it becomes much easier. As you may have guessed, our house had several more rooms than our new condo has. The young couple who bought our house did not own nearly enough furniture to fill the rooms, and they were as delighted to buy what we didn't want as we were to sell or give to them. This made the move much easier for all of us. Our trash; their treasures.

Make no mistake: downsizing is no walk in the park. Cleaning out a lifetime of memories is difficult. But I have to say, when it's done, it's a good feeling. My husband and I actually felt lighter and less burdened once the task was done. What's more, we don't miss any of it.

My husband has since died. Our last two years together were dominated by the realization of our worst fears as his terrible illness took over our lives. We were eternally grateful that the happy memories of our family home were safely in our hearts and not a burden on our backs. We were so pleased that we had been clever enough to have done our downsizing while we were still able to share both its work and its pleasure.

Jackie K of Jenkintown, Pennsylvania, had this take on downsizing:

As you downsize, you continue to grow. It's kind of like pruning a tree: you branch out in new directions! What a beautiful thought! What we sometimes forget is that we are always creating new and beautiful things that we share with family and friends.

WHO GETS THE STUFF WE GIVE AWAY?

Certainly this is one of the knottiest problems. Some women have told us that whenever they broach the subject to their children (dividing up our things after we die), the children don't want to discuss it. It's as hard for them as it is for us. **Carol V** of Philadelphia, Pennsylvania, not one to sweep tough decisions under the rug, approached it in this way:

> *There are other reasons for downsizing beyond need or necessity. And it's still not a walk in the park! We have "stuff" of both sentimental value and monetary value. I realized that someone would be wise to tackle it head on rather than leave the job to children who might not have a clue what the valuable things were worth or find it a burden to have to do it at all.*
>
> *Most painful was getting insurance coverage to be able to get estimates from prospective buyers, only to learn that the really good stuff was worth very little on the market. I did not like owning one valuable diamond ring (my mother's) that was indivisible: two daughters, five grandchildren; this did not feel right no matter what we decided. Well, it turned out one daughter wanted it very badly for both sentimental reasons, and the desire to see to it that her children would have it (kept in the family!), so that proved to be the best choice. I'm making it up to the other daughter in other ways to compensate for the great disparity in economic value.*

Almost all the women we spoke to told us that this is often the issue that they find the hardest to deal with. Many have said that this aspect of breaking up the house is the deal-breaker. They simply refuse to face it.

> *The most pleasant decision re "money stuff" had to do with the necessity to rewrite our wills. Vetting new lawyers was no fun, but one decision I made was a pleasure. I decided to give, in different forms, the money that I might have left to each grandchild to them directly during my lifetime instead. We have two older grandchildren who are both working. I set up Roth IRAs for them: a tad complicated, but they were thrilled. I recommend this to anyone who has the ability to do so: the bequest/ gift that keeps on giving.*

The foregoing unloading of stuff was so exhausting that I quit, leaving the disposition of the generations of china/silver/ tchotchkes to others. Not my problem. . . . Has anyone really enjoyed this type of thing? I did enjoy the Roth IRA gambit.

Carol divided the big things and left the lesser items for her children to deal with. Unfortunately, this sometimes leads to dissension among the siblings, possibly due more to unresolved family issues than to the financial or emotional worth of the items themselves.

WHAT DO WE KEEP?

Actually, downsizing becomes burdensome because indiscriminate accumulation is something that plagues some of us all our lives. **Shirley L** wrestled the problem with all good intentions and won! But here's what happened next:

Downsizing my four-story building and gallery was one mammoth endeavor, and having to do it alone was surely no picnic. But what is amazing is that after you have tossed, given, and sold off the "stuff," and you feel so good, you suddenly discover that you are at it again—adding more "stuff" to your life! And that's what happened to me. The book shelves are full again, the tchotchkes are all over the place. . . . Must be some sorta disease!

Deborah B, a blogger from Britain, will be in the ranks of the next generation of ElderChicks, but she has decided to plan ahead for her bout with downsizing. Let's hope she's more successful than Shirley L is.

I'm not ready to downsize yet, but that's no reason not to think about what we really need and what we don't! We are definitely "hoarders," and our loft is full of boxes the children have left behind or that we haven't unpacked since moving here to this large, rambling home over eight years ago.

You have inspired me to make a start so that when the day comes, if the day comes, that we have to say goodbye to the family home, we can do so without hiring a fleet of lorries to take stuff away.

At the moment, with five children—three sort of still living with us here and grandchildren on the way, I think we could do with the extra space a good clear-out would provide!

Jan T has a unique way of dealing with too much stuff. Maybe this will work for some of you:

I like the idea of living with less, but the reality of actually letting go is difficult for me. I have to downsize with baby steps. When I get motivated, I use the rule of five. Every day I have to get rid of five items. Initially it is pretty easy, but by day four it gets a little more challenging. Some weeks I will focus on one area of the house . . . for example, the laundry room or kitchen. This strategy has allowed me to be comfortable letting go of stuff. It is surprising how much progress you can make in a week with only five items a day.

Judith LeFevre of Marlton, New Jersey, is our downsizing expert. She does this for a living. In her workshops to help people who need help dealing with this challenge, she gives this professional advice:

Years go by, and we are all guilty of collecting items of distinct and indescribable value. The antique glasses from our great grandmothers, those silver trays that need to be polished or they'll turn black, the dress we wore ten years ago that will come back in style, or the photograph albums that contain the story of our children's lives. All of these things have importance, but when you are downsizing it is impossible to keep all of it with us. It is daunting to release these things into the wild abyss and possibly never see them again, but it is part of moving on and needs to be addressed with some TLC.

My first rule is never purge alone. Get a son, daughter, niece, best friend, or someone with a sense of clarity to help you. There are several steps to follow, as described below:

- **Do one section of the house at a time.** *Focus on one area before moving to the next. If you gather everything from the entire house up in one spot, you will be instantly overwhelmed.*

- **Start in your closet.** *If you have not worn an item in two years, take it to Goodwill, where a needy person will be glad to have it. That includes shoes, handbags, and those dressy dresses that we know are coming back in style but never really do. Pack as you go in plastic bags, then drive them immediately to the drop-off before you start changing your mind.*

- **Check out your kitchen.** *How many sets of dishes do you need? By the time we are ready to downsize, one set of dishes (service for eight) is more than enough. Have no more glasses than you need for everyday drinking and, of course, your wine glasses. Pots and pans are important if you are planning to do a lot of cooking. Pick the ones you use the most and give the rest away, including all of those serving pieces that are in the back of the cabinet. If you are entertaining a large group, use plastic dishware, glasses, and silverware. Who wants to clean up all those dishes anyway? (I bet a family member would love your china and crystal.)*

- **Look at your furniture.** *Can you see all of it in your new home? Remember, less is more. If you are moving to a smaller space and crowd it with furniture, you won't feel comfortable. Pick your favorite pieces to take with you, and add a few new ones if you can to make your new home feel like it was designed for you. Have a garage sale. Place some signs out in the neighborhood because your neighbors will be your best customers. If you are computer savvy and have* *some items that seem valuable, list them on eBay or take them to a consignment shop. (And there are always local companies that specialize in home sales.)*

Judith's final word of advice to downsizers is this:

Always ask three questions about your possessions:

- *Do I really love it?*
- *Do I really want it?*
- *Do I really need it?*

If you love the painting that you purchased in the summer of 1985, then keep it because you will find a place for it somewhere. If you want something but are not sure if you will ever use it, put it in the large carton labeled "Ask the Kids." If they take it to use at their home, you won't feel so bad. If they don't want it, give it away. If you need it or think you do, ask yourself when was the last time you used this. Can't remember? Then put it in the carton marked "Garage Sale."

To all of you making life changes, all I can say is don't fear the unknown. You will find that smaller homes give you a sense of freedom. I have been a realtor for many years, having left the corporate world to make the change. Change is good, so embrace it.

We talked with a group of city dwellers in Philadelphia, one of whom was a ninety-two-year-old retired dentist, **Bernard E**, who had moved from the suburbs in recent years, about what they had discovered about the process and outcomes of downsizing. As always, when seniors get together, they are worth listening to.

- **Joan P**: *Not only are we finding it more comfortable to be on one floor, we are socializing so much more because we see our neighbors and talk with them instead of going from the* *garage to the house. So getting rid of things has opened us up to a whole new life.*

- **Sue C**: *I was very hurt when my family didn't want things I loved and wouldn't have room for. I finally decided to put some things in storage for a year to get used to the idea of giving them away. That helped when I realized that I was living without them very well.*

- **Connie G**: *Some of them do want your treasures. I find myself sitting there on holidays at my children's homes and watch my things coming out of their cabinets and closets. They bring back good memories and give me a feeling of continuity in the family.*

- **Mary W**: *My kids had a great idea when my mother was going to sell her house and perhaps many of the things in it. They made a video of their Gran walking through the whole house, describing things they had always seen there and telling them about their origins. Now they have a record of her with a bit of oral history to preserve precious memories.*

- **Fran G**: *I rarely buy gifts anymore. Whenever I have to give one, and sometimes when I don't, I give away something from my home that I care about. (Otherwise, I wouldn't feel it meant anything as a gift!) Of course, I try to give it to a person who would appreciate the sentiment behind the gift—preferably something they've admired. It's a small way of downsizing—or at least of divesting.*

- **Bernard E**: *When my wife died after seventy years of a wonderful marriage, I moved from a large house to a small apartment, which meant that I had to dispose of so many things, including art that I loved and would have no room for. My son and daughter and their families had first dibs, of course, but much was still left, and we had a sale in the* *house. One woman admired a lithograph I had bought many years ago. I like it so much I had kept it in my office for years, where I would see it every day when I went to work. She asked me how much I would take if she were to buy it. I said I'd think about it—and check its present value. She came back again and told me that the artist was very famous, although she had never heard of him. I told her that I knew that, and that I knew its market value was between $1,500 and $2,000. She said she'd have to think about it. When she came back a third time, I gave it to her. I had thought about it, too. And I decided it meant more to me to have it belong to someone who clearly loved it as I did than to have the money.*

At ninety-eight, **Thelma G** of Redwood City, California, has established new homes many times—from a large, historic five-bedroom house in New England to successively smaller digs until reaching her latest small apartment. When we interviewed Thelma, we saw that the apartment was made beautiful by her own artwork, ceramics, and upholstery and drapes. Shedding what she no longer needs has become easier over the years. And this is what we learned: *Thelma's apartment is inspiring because it reflects what remains important to her in the material world and it mirrors the spirit and positive energy with which she still approaches life.*

TIME TO BITE THE BULLET

The subject of downsizing drew the greatest response of any topics raised at our workshops, Lunch and Listens, individual interviews, and during the blog's existence. So many of us are forced by circumstance to do it, and so many others would choose to avoid leaving the job to others. And, of course, so many things carry emotional weight that decisions to keep or not to keep can sometimes bring us to tears. However, in this chapter you've met people who have downsized it and continue to do it successfully. We've learned that the most successful downsizers are people who appreciate what they achieve by unburdening themselves of possessions they no longer need and realize the relief and sense of freedom and space they gain.

Warning: Just don't do what Shirley did—unless you just can't help it, of course.

5

THE CHILDREN ARE ADULTS

Has the Family Dynamic Outgrown Issues of Control, Rebellion, and Sibling Rivalry? How Do We Keep a Sense of Family over Generations?

The family—that octopus from whose tentacles we never quite escape, nor, in our inmost hearts, ever quite wish to.
—Dodie Smith

More transitions!

When we were in charge of our families, we called the shots, we made the rules, we imparted and imposed our values. The household was our creation. The atmosphere, the mood, the ambience, the tone were set by us. We dealt with our need to protect and provide, our intense love, our dreams and expectations for our children. We coped with sibling rivalry, adolescent rebellion, raging hormones. Our investment in this family has been huge.

Now our children have grown up. The family has branched out. Separations have occurred, some happy, some unwelcome. Regardless of the circumstances, the family is still the core of our being. However, mutual needs of our family members have changed, and the loci of control have shifted. How do we manage these new permutations of our family?

In our interviews, we found these general issues that women find troubling and needing to address:

- **It's hard to give up control.**
- **My children refuse to grow up!**
- **My children neglect me.**
- **My child is gay/lesbian.**
- **I'm worried about our children's families.**
- **Sibling rivalry, still unresolved.**
- **My children don't like my new partner.**

IT'S HARD TO GIVE UP CONTROL

Remember your first apartment? Mom liked beige. You preferred blue. She urged traditional. You considered only modern. You wanted to make your own choices, realizing that it was time for you to take control of your life. Your parents' opinions were welcome, but not final. Their financial help was accepted, but not demeaning. You convinced them that you were entitled to live your own life, and they readjusted their expectations, gradually letting go. Some tension, maybe a lot, was felt on both sides, but all to the good! The equation had changed, but you and your parents figured it out, and you were on your way toward a healthy, loving adult relationship in which friendship, not control, was the basis.

Unfortunately, the picture is not always so pretty. Some parents refuse to let their children grow up, trying to continue to exert influence on their choice of spouse, career, and lifestyle. These parents often impose guilt trips, feign illness, become angry and withdrawn, or threaten to estrange or disown their children. The possibilities are endless in families where relinquishing control does not occur, often crippling future relationships.

Adult children's responses to overcontrolling parents are equally creative and maybe even pathological. We've all seen our children roll their eyes and then do their own thing. But some children meekly accept and never grow up. Others become angry and rebellious, avoiding their parents as much as they can. The saddest of all are adult parent-child relationships that can only be described as barren and devoid of any intimacy. How awful those obligatory holiday reunions must be!

Thelma G of Redwood City, California, in her late nineties, described her sad relationship with her mother and tells of her resolve to apply what she had learned.

> My mother-daughter story has to begin with my mother and me. My mother was a very pretty woman with many wonderful talents for which she was admired. When people first met her they were intrigued by the vast amount of knowledge she had about so many things as well as the beauty of everything that she made. But their interest soon waned since she always freely offered her opinion and had to be right. She was able to converse about many interesting subjects, but others soon learned that to have an opinion of their own caused friction and that she had no sense of humor.
>
> The inevitable always happened: they no longer found Regina interesting and worth spending time with because it always became very uncomfortable and even ugly. There was only one way, hers. As a result, she never had friends, and her relationship with her mother—and me—was also very terrible. It was one of the hardest lessons for me to learn: how to be with Mama without getting into an argument and yet keep my integrity.
>
> The turning point in my relationship with Mama came after a very ugly scene when Jeannie was a teething infant and Mama

insisted that she hold the baby, who only screamed harder when Mama held her. After I took the baby from her, Mama screamed and carried on with abusive and hurtful language— mind you, none of which was cursing or vulgar. She was so hysterical that Daddy had a difficult time quieting her enough to take her home on the train. My son Peter was so upset that he called her a "bad grandma" and then ran to his room and cried himself to sleep. After a few days, during which I hoped she had calmed down, I called her, but she hung up when she heard my voice. Every few days I tried to speak to her, but without any success. All through those nine months Daddy kept in touch with me and urged me to be patient. He was sure that she was sorry for her behavior but found it extremely difficult to say she was sorry or even to just let it pass.

Eventually, I conspired with my sister Ruthie to call at her house when Mama was visiting and put Peter on the phone to invite her to his fourth birthday party. When she came to the phone, Peter invited her, but she said that couldn't she come on that day, so he invited her for Thanksgiving dinner (the follow- ing week), and she accepted. I was a nervous wreck waiting for them to drive up to our door, and just before their arrival, while taking the turkey from the oven I let the pan slip, and the turkey bounced out onto the floor. My friend and neighbor, Alice, was there, and she quickly helped clean the mess while I kept everyone at the front door with prolonged greetings. The ice had been broken, and there never was a word spoken about the event, but from that time on she and I became very close. After a while I found that I no longer had to weigh and meas- ure every word or feel that I was "walking on eggshells."

The night before she died, I dreamed that she had died, and when I woke up I told my husband. Later that day, I got a call from a friend, who had been notified by the police that Mama's body was being held in the city morgue as unidentified. She had dropped dead in Woolworth's five-and-dime store. I had been trying all day to call her but got no answer. The police had found my friend's number in Mama's purse, and the friend helped locate Daddy and me. After the funeral, Daddy remembered that we always used to tease Mama and say that the old Scottish hymn, "Lord, grant that I may always be right, for thou knowest I am hard to turn" was only true for her when it stopped after "I am" . . . because she didn't believe that she was hard to turn! No one can say that she didn't try or that she was mean-spirited. She aspired to the highest and wanted everyone to set their goals for the highest points, and she expected that everyone had the same standards and aspirations.

Mama had so many wonderful qualities that one couldn't put down and just toss aside. Not only was she artistic, with a great sense of design and color, she was able to execute her ideas on paper and cloth. She was an avid reader, and her range of educational and informational material was wide, and she researched new ideas in various fields. Her ideas of a healthy diet came from her investigation of the materials she had read. As a result, we were introduced to a diet that at that time was considered odd, to say the least. It was a rare occasion that we had fried foods, and she was ever on guard when it came to sugar. She cut down on the amount of sugar in every recipe, a practice I still follow. I had never been much of a candy eater and in my adult life didn't buy any—I might eat it only if it is put before me. When we were children and had a piece of candy we were immediately sent to brush our teeth, and that took all the wonderful taste right out of our mouths. I think that memory was always in my mind when candy was put before me, and all that would come into my mouth was the taste of Colgate's toothpaste.

While I admired all her talents, I had a very difficult time relating to her on a mother-daughter level until just two years before her death. I'm so grateful that we were able to put aside all the difficult years and enjoy each other's company. I'm sure that the lessons I learned from that helped me avoid problems with my children. Jeannie and I have had a loving friendship throughout our lives and one that I gratefully cherish. I wish every mother had a relationship with her daughter like I

have—one filled with respect, without intruding on each oth-
er's lives, always supportive and ready to help when needed. In
truth, a loving friendship.

We met with a group of women at one of our Lunch and Listen
meetings and posed this question of control to them. They had
much to offer.

- **Jane D's** mother advised her that a good mother-in-law
  keeps her mouth shut and wears beige.

- **Esther R's** mother advised her to keep her mouth shut and
  her purse open.

- **Elena S's** mother always told her what to do. "Once my
  mother told me to wear a coat because it's raining. I said to
  her, 'Mom, I'm forty years old. I know what I should wear.'
  She looked at me and said, 'You're forty?'"

But don't think that these women are patsies in their own families. Despite their sage advice, it became apparent that they all
preside over families with youngsters-turned-adults and have giv-
en much thought to their changing role in the family dynamic.
Most agree that honesty requires that they offer suggestions and
opinions when they feel it will help in a tough situation. Where it
doesn't really matter, where it's a matter of style or form, they
keep an open mind and are accepting. They all agree that the
secret of speaking their mind is a light touch and a judicious
selection of issues. No one welcomes a ton of bricks, least of all
their adult children, and no one takes kindly to a barrage of unwelcome ideas.

On the other hand, this was delivered almost without a pause
for breath at another of our Lunch and Listen sessions. You will
understand why the eighty-something woman who said the following wishes to remain anonymous:

Here is my question:

How come we are the generations of mothers—and so far I have discovered this is true of many of my friends—who never argue or disagree—but always go along with whatever our kids say? It's always "That's a wonderful idea," or "That really looks good," and "I love what you did with this room," while really hating it.

We pussyfoot around, hesitating to really tell it like we see it. But to our friends we speak truthfully and frankly, as in "I hate your haircut." How come we can't be truthful with our grown kids? What makes us not want to confront them? And when we forget ourselves, sometimes letting out a "Why in the world did you do that?" we live to regret it. How come? Not wanting to rock the ship?

All constructive criticism is given in very good faith. How come it's not received that way? Does it have something to do with the genes? Is it passed down from mom to mom? Don't think so, don't remember my mom hesitating about anything. Is it a generational attitude? Just wondering. How come?

So much has to do with how criticism is delivered and the relationship you have with your adult children. Strong relationships can weather strong disagreements. Arguments are never pleasant affairs and have nothing to do with generations. It's no secret that constructive suggestions or mild disagreements are not as emotion laden and will usually enjoy a better reception. Speaking the truth as you see it should not damage a relationship unless it is really a constant harangue.

But when you offer unsolicited criticism to people, know that you are risking their displeasure, whatever their age, whatever their relationship to you. Try to see yourself from your children's perspective. Do you tell them how much you respect the adults they've become, and do you respect their right to run their lives as they see fit? Or are you generally a disapproving person, critical of so much they do? Sometimes we need to look inward. How do you feel if the criticism is directed at you? Is it welcome, or does it sting?

MY CHILDREN REFUSE TO GROW UP

More often than not, you've set aside your own needs and wants to cater to your children's. The kids are grown, and now you are ready to turn your attention to yourself—you've got the time and energy. Your mother may not have had the expectation that new excitements and interests could challenge her in this vital phase of her life once the nest emptied. Your attitude is different from hers. You've got a lot of living to do!

You've pushed the reset button on your maternal responsibilities. You love your kids a lot and want to expand and extend your relationship with them. Now you are all adults who respect each other's decisions and space as mutually loving adults do. Are your kids ready for this? Sometimes they're not. Here's what **Cindy M** from Charleston, South Carolina, told us:

> *My children are in their early thirties, have jobs, live independently, are both single and not currently involved in serious relationships. They were both needy as children because of issues that are now pretty much resolved. My daughter was adopted, and this, of course, must have had an effect on her which was different from the experience of my biological son, who had serious health issues, some of which persist to this day. We were very concerned parents. I was a very watchful mother. We read everything we could get our hands on, consulted with professionals, were completely devoted to them, and I believe we cared for their physical and emotional needs well.*

My husband died when our children were in their early twenties, and this was a severe blow to us all. How to cope with adult children who had extra issues as children, adolescents, and now as young adults, was a puzzle to me. In reflection, I realize that my own mother, who is still alive, could not be a role model for me. She had lost her parents before she was twenty, never had older parents to deal with, and never had needy adult children to deal with, either. By the time I had turned twenty-two, I was married and gone from my parents' house. When my parents offered me their home following the divorce of my first husband, I said, "No thanks! I'll be fine!" The last thing I wanted to do was go back to live with my parents. By the time I was my son's age, I was in a second marriage, had a degree, a job, a pension plan, medical benefits, a house, and two children.

So here I am now, adrift at sixty-three with two kids in their thirties and no dad. Just their mom. Yes, they are somewhat needier than most, but they are thirty and must learn to cope in their world. I feel it is time for me to give up that high alert that we lived on as they were growing up. Maybe I should have done it sooner. I can't fix everything. I can empathize, but I can't do it for them.

I have, after several years, become involved in a serious relationship. My kids and he got along well. However, my children tell me that they feel neglected because I am no longer always available. "No longer available" means I balk at cooking for them and their friends, lending my car at any time regardless of my plans, or helping them solve their personal problems whenever they ask. I had to sit them down and issue my declaration of independence:

And so I told them this: **I'm still your mom—but I am no longer your mommy.**

"You are adults. You have grown-up lives to lead: careers to develop, your place in the world to stake out, relationships to cement, paths to determine. It's time for you to break free.

"I know you've had issues in your lives. Everyone has 'issues.' When you're thirty, you need to find ways to deal with them. You can't rely on mommy to fix everything anymore. I'll always be here when you need an ear or maybe some advice which you must feel free to take or leave. But I'm no longer the fixer-in-chief. You have to be in control.

"And there's something else. I wouldn't mind if you offered to do something for me sometimes. I wouldn't mind if you invited me to your house for dinner or asked me to join you doing something 'adult.' Call me, text me, e-mail me, set a date, let's take a walk. My mommy days of cooking and cleaning for you are over! I have a life of my own now. I don't want to run my schedule according to your schedules."

It's not that they're selfish. They are good, loving kids and I like spending time with them. But they have been living comfortably in a pattern that I've changed—and they've noticed that I'm no longer in the mommy business. I made a shift in my life when I sold the family home and I didn't ask their permission. They are happy for me, and they do like that I'm not dependent on them. I'm sure their neediness will work itself out. But I had to sit them down and spell it out! They've already shown that they are beginning to respect my boundaries. They seem to recognize that I've hung up my mommy hat. I think this whole blowup will end happily and benefit us all.

MY CHILDREN CAN'T TAKE CARE OF THEIR CHILDREN

We met **Gerrie G** at a senior center located in an old, dreary building in Philadelphia, Pennsylvania, where everything seems to be greatly in need of paint. The décor is shabby, and all the tired, mismatched, probably donated items of furniture are assigned a use somewhere. The people are elderly, many in wheelchairs or with walkers, casually dressed, and appear to be of very modest means. There is amid this rather grim backdrop, however, a buzz of affability and activity. It feels like a happy place. Are all these seniors merely whistling in the dark? Making lemonade? Well, some are and some are not.

Gerrie sat primly among a group of men and women—about twenty in all—who gather every Tuesday morning at the senior center to exchange ideas about almost everything. We were there to lead a discussion group, to hear their thoughts about how they see themselves fitting into the world around them and how they feel the world fits into their lives. Time was limited, and some people had lots they wanted to contribute. When the session was over, it had been far too short, they complained. They said they were not often asked about their thoughts and there was much more to say. We were invited back. Gerrie told us this:

> When I knew I had to be the one to raise my grandson, I was thinking I'm too old for this! For the first time I began to feel my age. I had already raised my children and now here I was, doing the parent thing again. My daughter was whacked out on drugs, not able to take care of her own child, and someone had to save this innocent babe. So I quit my job, stepped up, and you know what? My life got richer.

> My daughter's child was born out of wedlock, and I raised him. He was my heart. Still is! My daughter was there—and not there, if you know what I mean. She was very troubled. My grandson is now thirty-two. My daughter has since learned from her mistakes and has become a wonderful person. She made a complete change. After my husband died, she and I lived together in my home. She went to work, and I took care of her son.

> I don't know why my daughter, when she was younger, gave in to so many of the temptations that almost ruined her life. My life was so different. My first job was at Sears, typing labels on the packages that went out. I enjoyed working. Then the war came—World War II. I was offered a job working with key-punch cards, but I wasn't sure I could do it, so I turned it

down. On the way out, I saw that everyone working there was white. And I thought, "If those white girls can do this, so can I." I asked if it was too late to change my mind and was told it's never too late. So I learned to operate the IBM machinery, and I stayed on that job until I got married. The war was still on, my husband was in the service, and I continued to work. We had two children—two boys—and after each one was born, I quit for a while to take care of them and then found a new job with the government.

But I divorced my husband. I was young when I married Richard, married him right out of school. He was my first love. But when he came back from the war, he was different. Now we know about posttraumatic stress, but we didn't know about that then. I was too immature to understand. I couldn't cope with some of the things he would want to talk about. I regret that. I don't think I would have broken up with my first husband if I had had a better mind than I did.

Well, I married again. A good man, and we had a son and a daughter. I loved him, and he worked hard and took care of me. I think he made me what I am today. But I don't think I ever let my first husband really get out of my life.

I worked after each child was born. I had mostly government jobs that required exams. I have always liked a challenge. My last job was on the banking floor at PSFS, and I worked there for twenty-one years until I retired to take care of my husband and my grandson.

I saved some money out of every paycheck and always snuck some out of my house money. My second husband wasn't a saver but I always was, and I managed to own three houses at the same time. My husband was a good man but did not know how to manage money, so I took charge.

I gave one of my houses to the grandson I raised. But I gave it to him before he was old enough to be responsible, and he lost it because of a bad financial dealing. That really hurt because my husband and I really struggled to buy those houses. I turned another home over to my daughter, and she's using that for underprivileged women who live there until they can get back on their feet. She's doing really well with that.

My daughter, as I told you, was addicted to drugs when she was young, but she's made a big turnaround in her life. I like that she's helping women who themselves are having a bad time. You can see how she's turned her life around. She works hard at her job and also manages this home for troubled women. We live together now in the third house, and we get along very well. I am very glad that I stepped up when she needed me to raise her child. I was very resentful at the time, but I felt I had no choice. We all got past that, and we're all all right now.

Gerrie is a woman without anger and without malice. She brings to her senior life all the dignity, reflection, and spirit that accompanied her throughout life. She is willing to face the decisions she has made that turned out to be wrong and is pleased about the things she feels she has done right. Gerrie has never shied from the truth and continues to maintain a sensible perspective about herself and how she fits into the world.

MY CHILDREN NEGLECT ME

But then we heard the other side of the coin—the moms who feel their children are neglecting them.

I am a widow of twenty years, in good health and leading an active life. I have loved being with, doing for, helping out, taking out, and staying overnight with my grandchildren. I do notice now that half of them have reached their mid teens . . . hmm, how should I say this . . . I get fewer calls from my daughters because they no longer need the things I outlined above. My weekends are suddenly half empty, no calls, no re-quests for help. Well, what about me now?

This woman, who also wanted her name withheld, is not alone. Quite a few expressed their feelings of rejection once they were no longer needed in ways they were accustomed to giving. Here is another example of what we heard. We are pleased that Lunch and Listen offered this woman sisterhood and fellowship. This was her response to the woman above:

Thank you, thank you . . . you hit the nail on the head . . . and your words validated what I often feel. It helps so much. . . . They still love me and care for me, but they don't recognize my loneliness. Thank you for pointing out I am not alone. I feel so much better . . . and I'm extremely glad I stumbled upon you ElderChicks.

And yet another:

My children are making the assumption that I can be left in limbo until I have a need. A need usually involves a medical emergency. I have to keep reminding myself that this is natural and to not harbor hurt feelings. I realize they are busy with their lives, and I accept that. They live in two separate cities. I am selfishly thinking, as I am widowed and live alone, how can they possibly forget to just call without a purpose or to phone me on a holiday? It is as if I have been filed in the "not-important-but-if-needed-I-will-help-out" folder. I miss their companionship. I do not know how to voice my feelings to them without making them feel guilty—which would make me unhappy also.

Here are some wise suggestions for women who feel neglected by their children:

- **Robin J** of Mobile, Alabama: *Be grateful for being in good health and active. Though I find myself in the same situation and feel irritated when others do not validate my loneliness and feelings of emptiness, my expectations of people and traditions that I thought I could count on have changed. No anger, just understanding for myself that life goes in separate directions than those we expected. I felt loss as I recognized these changed expectations, but life is not for looking back on what was or what might have been. It is enough to love each day for itself and for all the good things it brings.*

  We are still alive and able to enjoy small things without distraction. Peacefulness and acceptance give new appreciation for my own abilities. I feel triumphant in smaller things and look around me for new avenues of exploration. Silly as it may sound, I used to feel so dependent on so many loved ones to make me happy. I felt that unless someone was there, my joys were diminished. It isn't true. That I know now. So I am still ready for adventure, but the understanding that my life has changed gives new meaning to the word.

- **Hannah H** of Sarasota, Florida: *We must relish the years we have had with our children and grandchildren . . . acknowledge that they have lives of their own. Things change. With good health, energy, and interests, the time has come to share our abilities and compassion with the larger community. Volunteer! Help out at day-care facilities! Mentor a child at the neighborhood school. Have lunch and conversations (bitching is allowed) with friends! Join a health club or a nonprofit organization! There is so much out there. Give! Enjoy! It's up to you to make each day beautiful.*

- **Jackie K** of Jenkintown, Pennsylvania: *You are so ripe for volunteer work! Find something you like, and offer your services. It will make you feel fulfilled and others, too.* **Good luck!**

- **Lois Roelofs**: *I'll be hoping that you find an outlet for all that "giving" that's bursting for a place to go! There are many lonely kids and adults who would love to be on the receiving end.*

We sense the anger and bewilderment of these women who feel bereft. They are all justified, and their feelings should be acknowledged by their families. But now it's time to move on and look for ways to make their lives worthwhile by extending their energies and talents beyond the family. There are a lot of people out there who need us. We women must take this as an opportunity, not a threat, and become role models for our children and grandchildren. One day they will be "seniors." They will respect us all the more for it.

MY CHILD IS GAY/LESBIAN

Kay B of Austin, Texas had a different situation to report. Her granddaughter "came out of the closet" at age eighteen to the particular dismay of her mother. The new revelation further compounded already existing family difficulties. In this case, a wise and loving grandmother in her seventies came to the rescue. Here is Kay's story:

> *Jamie was always a difficult child. As a child, she had some health issues, her parents divorced when she was ten, and she was always painfully shy. It seemed that she and her mother (my daughter-in-law) were always at loggerheads. I was frequently disappointed that Jamie's mother seemed insensitive to Jamie's pain and even sometimes "used" her to get back at her ex-husband. Jamie was always special to me from the time she was a little girl because I felt she was the most vulnerable and neediest of my grandchildren.*

As shocked as I was to learn that she was a lesbian and that her mother essentially told her to "get over it," I knew that this young woman couldn't take another blow to her ego. I made her know that I loved and respected her and did not find her "damaged" or imperfect. This took some soul searching on my part because I had to get over some deep-seated prejudices of my own as well as be her champion to the rest of the family, many of whom were not so accepting.

I've watched her grow into a beautiful and talented young woman. I saw myself grow up, too, as I swallowed hard and accepted her without judging her. My husband and I have a very close and loving relationship with Jamie and her partner, both of whom we cherish. They have greatly enriched our lives.

Set in her ways? Too old to change? No way! This story is a tribute to Kay's ability to reevaluate her attitudes, to think, feel, and act in a way that goes counter to some of her long and dearly held beliefs. She focused on the person, not on the dogma. Kay resisted and broke the stereotype about aging—the one about the old dog and the new tricks. This is what we mean when we talk about changing cultural stereotypes about aging.

We know that families come in all shapes and sizes. Here is one we met that has dealt with dramatic changes in its own way:

Mary Margaret D of Washington, DC, the second-oldest of seven children, grew up in a happy, loving family with lots of room for her tomboy activities with brothers and, as she puts it, lots of early driving experience. Their old farmhouse provided opportunity for the four brothers and three sisters to work with their dad on the constant repairs and renovation it needed, with the result that she laid the foundation for skills she has developed and used in fixing anything that needed fixing in her own and other people's houses. She was a fifteen-year-old high school student when her Catholic girls' high school recruited boys from the nearby boys' school for a play and she met Joe.

> *Luckily we went to the same party, and he had the most won-derful mind. We could talk for hours. My family loved him, too. There was never anyone else after we met. We married eight years later. My father died suddenly in January, before the May of our scheduled wedding, which was devastating. So we postponed it and had a double wedding with my sister in September.*

Mary Margaret's and Joe's college years, hers in a truncated nurs-ing education followed by an unfinished university period, and his followed by military service, were interruptions before their wed-ding in 1966. With Joe's encouragement, she was to go back to school and finish her degree as he started work and graduate school. Almost immediately, as it's said today, "*they* were preg-nant."

For the most part, life was good. They invested in properties, which she personally renovated. They loved each other. Their children were flourishing. They had close attachments to family and friends. Fast forward to 1989, with their daughter and son both in college, and Mary Margaret and Joe about to go to Eu-rope to accompany a choral group in which her brother was sing-ing, and Joe fell ill with a non-life-threatening illness. He insisted Mary Margaret go ahead, and she did.

> *On that trip, I experienced what the French would call a* coup de foudre: *an immediate attraction that hit like a bolt of light-ning. I fell in love with someone I met in that group. The big surprise was that the person was a woman, a lesbian, more than ten years my junior.*

Had you ever felt that kind of attraction for another wom-an?

No. But looking back, I think others saw something in me. I had crushes on nuns as a girl, but most girls did—and they weren't sexual. I think now that some of the women who were asking me to have dinner or a drink with them after the gym might have had an intuition. I even think my mother may have been particularly encouraging of my marrying because I was such a tomboy, unlike my sisters. And most surprising to me was my daughter's reaction: "Oh, Mom, I knew."

At home, we had already begun the process of selling our house in the suburbs and moving into the city, so a disruption of how we lived had already begun when Joe and I told the children we were getting divorced. He asked me not to tell them the real reason yet, which I think was wrong, but I agreed and waited for several months while, I think, he adjusted to the idea.

Today, Mary Margaret's family has a loving relationship that has expanded to include her partner, Angela—herself the youngest of five sisters and the daughter of a ninety-one-year-old mother who not only accepts Mary Margaret but appreciates and loves her. Mary Margaret's four little granddaughters call Angela "Nana." Joe is close to all. Despite her great fear of loss over twenty years ago, Mary Margaret's husband, children, their spouses, her siblings, and her close friends have been, as always, her support as she is theirs.

I'M WORRIED ABOUT OUR CHILDREN'S FAMILIES

- How are they are raising our grandchildren?

- I'm not crazy about my son- or daughter-in-law.

- Uh-oh! My kids have live-in partners.

- I'm worried about their nontraditional lifestyles.

- How do I get along with their blended families?

- The divorce is harming the children.

Don't they know that kids have to go to bed at a decent hour? That they should eat something besides noodles for breakfast, lunch, and dinner? And what about that boyfriend that sleeps with their mother? How do they explain that? Daddy's home cleaning and cooking while mommy goes to work? What kind of a role model is that for my grandsons? The children are being harmed by the divorce.

"Is *anything* all right?" we've sometimes wanted to ask in our travels and interviews. So they're not doing it the way you did! So you think they're not doing it right! Well, maybe that's true and maybe it's not. The point is you will not be helping your relationship with your adult children by interfering. Here are some dos and don'ts:

- Do let them benefit from your wisdom—*only if you're asked!*

- Do *listen* when they want to talk.

- When you ask questions, *really listen* to their answers.

- Do try to see things from their perspective.

- Do try to be tolerant and accepting.

- Do respect their adult right to live as they see fit.

- Don't give advice if none is requested.

- Don't roll your eyes at their mates or significant others.

- Don't purse your lips at their sexual orientation.

- Don't tell them how to raise their kids.

- Don't show your disapproval.

- Don't judge them.

At one of our *Lunch and Listen* sessions, an otherwise very smart woman described her feeling of disappointment and disapproval when she saw her daughter, who had just arrived at the airport for a rare visit. **Evelyn H** of Cherry Hill, New Jersey, said, "I couldn't believe how she looked—positively unkempt! How can she travel looking like that—and she's a lawyer!" When the commiserating giggles died down, **Martha M** looked at Evelyn and said, "You didn't tell her that, did you?" "Of course, I did," Evelyn said, "I'm her mother and she needs to hear it."

Needs to hear it? Maybe that's a matter of judgment, and maybe that's why the visits are so rare.

SIBLING RIVALRY, STILL UNRESOLVED

The question is not whether sibling rivalry continues into adulthood. The question is: When do we stop thinking we can do anything about it?

When we reflect on our own feelings about our siblings, some of us have had the benefit of long, affectionate, caring relationships; others, not so much. Geographical distance, divisive in-laws, or remembered rivalries and hurts may have left marks that are hard to erase, even if we try to face the causes and attempt to resolve these nasty rifts. Most of us eventually recognize and accept what life has brought, even when an unbreakable bond, or so we assumed, is broken.

Yet when we observe our adult offspring, we realize that family dynamics can range from close, loving, and supportive to outright anger and hostility. When antagonism takes over, we wonder where *we* went wrong and yearn to restore harmony. Even when harmony wasn't so evident when our children were really children, we always thought they would surely outgrow their squabbling ways and "always have each other."

Roberta S of Arlington, Virginia, told us how she felt about her grown daughters who had a serious falling out.

> *So Robin fired off some e-mails that let fly her resentment at years of being second banana in the Steinfeld bunch. Boy, did I ever empathize with that! My older brother was a bear sometimes as I was growing up. From the time she was a little girl, big sister Amy practiced and perfected the tyranny of the older sib. Well, as an adult, Robin finally acknowledged these old feelings of hurt and said some things to Amy that hurt her. Back and forth went the e-mails, and both got in deeper—"You said! I said! Who said what first!"*
>
> *I longed to scream at these grown daughters, "If you can't play nice, go to your rooms!" These are two outstanding women. They're bigger than this.*
>
> *Robin now wants to put it behind her and move on. Amy prefers to remain hurt at Robin's accusations and nurse her anger. As parents, we offered outside mediation to help them resolve their issues. Amy was willing to air this in front of a third party. Robin wasn't ready. Then Robin was agreeable and Amy wasn't. Both finally agreed to mediation but, unfortunately, it failed. Robin's solution is to put the hurts behind, move on, and save the family. Amy feels she is owed an apology before she will consider reconciliation.*
>
> *I understand both their positions, sort of. That's what I understand in my head. But this is what I feel in my heart. I feel as though my heart is being torn from my breast because Amy has decided to "divorce" her sister. I consider this my failure.*
>
> *My failure in this as a mother is that I thought—and still think—that sibling rivalry is a normal part of growing up. That it would pass with adulthood. That the strength of the family bond would outweigh the hurts of childhood. I know that in every family we deal with really strong feelings. There's love, hate, pride, jealousy, fun, guilt. Let's see, what else? We feel compassion, anger, weakness, fear, anxiety. Did I leave*

*anything out? Probably. But the strongest thing we feel is kin-
ship. We're all in this together.*

*I even thought—and still think—that working out sibling ri-
valries teaches kids perspective and helps them face the world,
maybe better prepared to deal with what they will find out
there when they're grown up. After all, the world is filled with
wonderful stuff but also with cruelty and indifference. And
family members know they can count on each other when there
is need because each of us has felt and handled all of these good
and bad feelings. None of us in the family is above reproach.
With all our faults and virtues, it's a comfort to know that our
family loves, cares, and accepts us—that we stand together.*

*Well, the family has managed to stay together—except for
Amy, who remains apart. My husband and I find each of our
four children and their spouses/partners wonderful and special
in their own ways. The grandchildren are magical to us and
have all grown into delicious human beings. We are especially
grateful that the cousins have managed to remain close despite
the difficulties some of their parents are experiencing. We find
it comforting that the third generation remains whole.*

Roberta told us that she has a great relationship with all her
children and grandchildren. She has finally faced the fact that this
matter is out of her control. She realizes she can't correct it, and
so with time she has finally reached some acceptance. She still
wonders, however, where she went wrong as a parent.

Mary G of Bethesda, Maryland, has been emotionally and
geographically distanced from her only sister for many years.
Mary told us that she finally has come to grips with her hurt. Now
both in their late seventies, she reflects:

*I suppose there are many reasons for her anger, but none
seems to me to be important enough to cause a break in the
bond of sisterhood. Why family means more to me than it does*

to her I cannot understand. I make an effort to keep in touch by phone occasionally. I know I wish her well and would love for things to be otherwise, but I recognize they never will be. I've tried, but I can't do anything about it. It took me a long time to accept this.

As with so much in life, it turns out that flexibility, resilience, and acceptance work wonders for the heart while rigidity, anger, and regret eat away at it. A tightly clenched fist becomes difficult to maintain. An open hand will be grasped with love.

MY CHILDREN DON'T LIKE MY NEW PARTNER

At one of our *Lunch and Listens*, the following exchange took place. They both asked that their names be withheld.

Anne: *My husband died a few years ago. I finally started dating, and now I've found a man I love and who loves me. My children are very distant, if not downright nasty to him. I don't know why. We haven't really talked about it because it's a very sensitive subject and I'm not comfortable talking to them about him. So I just keep everybody separated. We just don't do anything together. But I'd like him to be a part of the family and bring him to family functions. It can't go on this way, and I don't want to give him up.*

Andrea: *Well, I'm having the same problem. Since my divorce, my children have been very supportive of me until I developed an intimate relationship with another man. They say they just don't like him. I think it's because he's not their father and maybe they're punishing me by not accepting anyone I like. Well, that's their tough luck! I refuse to keep him separate from my family, but this is getting so unpleasant that I'm afraid he'll leave me. And I can't say I'd blame him.*

The exchange generated much empathy from the group but not much in the way of solutions. All agreed that Anne and Andrea are entitled to embracing, figuratively and literally, new men in their lives. And all agreed that the children are not acting like adults even though they have reached adulthood. Most suggestions to Anne were that she should confront the issue with her children and tell them in a tender way that she feels vulnerable, alone, in need of affection and intimacy, and really welcomes this man's attention, and also that she loves him and feels the love is mutual. The group felt that she should ask them to put their negative feelings aside and trust and respect that their mother has made a good choice. If they can't do that, they should at least button their lips.

Perhaps, the group thought, Andrea is too much "in their face," might soften her tone and explain what it means to her to have both this man and her family on her side—that she needs them both. Explain that this man is not replacing their father but fills a huge gap in her heart. Perhaps, if asked, the children can focus on their mother rather than on themselves.

The dynamics of a family with adult children! As parents, our job never ends. As the old saying goes: *Small children, small problems; big children, big problems.* Managing extended families, blended families, changing mores, revised gender roles, mobile societies, and unimagined lifestyles can be big problems. We are challenged daily to deal with these issues. The alternative is to retreat into our senior bubble, a subject explored in chapter 10.

6

I CAN'T USE MY COMPUTER—OR KNIT OR ROLLERBLADE

How Do I Push Myself to Learn New Skills? The World Is Changing around Me.—How Do I Remain Part of It?

If in the last few years you haven't discarded a major opinion or acquired a new one, check your pulse. You may be dead.
—Gelett Burgess

Oh, the exhausting pace of change!

We're not just imagining it; the pace really *is* faster than it was in our parents' generation. The twenty-four-hour news cycle, the whirlwind of ideas in the air, the sight of people in the streets talking to themselves! Wait a minute. They're not talking to themselves—they have buttons in their ears! They're talking on phones! Maybe that's why so few make eye contact anymore. They're wired, just like everything else seems to be. But I'm not. Is this still my world?

Believe it or not, it is. It's the only world we've got, and we're finding our own ways to live in it. Do we need to learn it all? Are we still able to learn new skills? Sometimes it looks as though there is so much that is new that we're exhausted just thinking about it. And then there's the fear that we may not be able to—especially when we observe five-year-olds pushing buttons on what looks like an iPhone. Even if it turns out the iPhone is only a toy, it still may be daunting in our eyes.

Now, take a deep breath and discover that help is on the way. It turns out that our brains have a reset button—kind of like the one on the computer, or if it's easier to think about, the one in the bowling lane. Most important and encouraging: we've actually been learning some of the new technology painlessly as it's crept into our daily lives. New learning is keeping our minds active, and brain studies show that the activity matters.

In chapter 9, **Gale C** of Boston, Massachusetts, talks about the medical library she set up in Cambodia after she retired from her career as a medical librarian in Boston. This ambitious project required that she learn new technology. Dramatic changes have been made in the way libraries and information are accessed during the past ten years. Gale was undaunted as she learned to use the Internet and the computer. The skills for which she had been trained were virtually obsolete by the time she set out to create the medical library.

> *For the first few years, I visited Cambodia three or four times a year to get the project under way. After that, only once a year most years. Now that the Internet is so available to all, we do much more communication via e-mail and the cybersphere. That's the reason I learned to use the computer. At first, faxing was the fast, techy way to go. With the explosion of the Internet, I had to become computer literate if I wanted to stay involved in the Cambodia project. In fact, I've had to update all my library skills in order to keep up with the way libraries function online these days. It seems I am constantly learning.*

Libby B of Oxnard, California, still working, remembers that a long time ago, these were her thoughts about all the new technology: "Wouldn't it be great if we could just stop the world for a year so the rest of us could catch up?" It turned out that she had to catch up and learn if she were to continue to practice law past her eighth decade. So she did. Many other women commented on the role of new technology in their lives:

- **Lois Roelofs**: *Thanks for another nudge toward an iPhone and e-reader. I've had a computer since they cost $4,000 (late 1980s), but I've been sluggish on the other things. Another advantage to being a bit tech savvy at our age is that I'm now organizing a fiftieth college reunion, and if all my former classmates were all on e-mail, it would be lots simpler! My seventy-four-year-old sister just got her first computer, and her first words were, "This is so much fun. I can look so many things up." Plus, she's enjoying sending and receiving photos for the first time.*

- **Suzan G** of Weston, Connecticut: *Recently, my husband and I received an iPad as an anniversary gift. Off we went to the Apple store, where we had reserved places in the class for iPad "beginners." We were the youngest participants, and we're in our early seventies! As we strive to embrace the new technology, I am reminded that we are mere tourists in that world, while those younger than we are true natives. But tourists can still learn a lot and have fun!*

  I did not know it then, but learning iPad skills eventually came to be a lifesaver for me. Last summer I broke my leg rather badly, and the iPad became my constant companion and link to the outside world. No matter how much pain I was in, at any time of the day or night I could pay my bills, write e-mails, and communicate with friends. The phrase "Adapt or die!" became my mantra. And I found that my new skills were transferable.

Recently, we bought a car that came with all kinds of new technology, including keyless entry, a GPS, and a myriad of navigational and entertainment accessories. Confronted with the new technology, my husband was less than enthusiastic with the voice-activated commands necessary to "simplify" the driving experience. But after much shouting and talking back to the helpful little lady who hides inside the dashboard and gives instructions on where to turn and which route to take, we have mastered the art of pushing buttons fearlessly, safe in the knowledge that the car will not explode. Our car, just like our iPad, has a picture of a little house on the dashboard. Who says you can't go home again? Pushing the "home" button erases all of our errors, and we gamely try again. The best part is we laugh at ourselves as we crawl into this new world of information technology.

- **Joan S**: *No reason to not keep on learning. . . . I'm eighty-one and regularly play Words with Friends on my cell phone with five different people. I bought Skype for my computer so I could really enjoy my first great grandchild. I am on Facebook and LinkedIn and check my business and personal e-mail a couple of times a day both on my computer and on my cell phone. Nothing annoys me more than my friends who still haven't mastered e-mail. It's so much harder to communicate little messages when everyone has to be on a phone. No excuses!*

But **Mary S** of Drexel Hill, Pennsylvania, demurred

iPads and smart phones may appeal to well-heeled seniors, but for those of us struggling to make our dwindling savings and unaugmented pensions (no COLAs for how long?) meet our needs as we age and become less able to produce income, they are just too damn expensive. Guess I'll have to wait till the prices come down. (I kind of like holding books, anyway, and I can write in the margins.)

According to Christina Bonnington, (Wired[1]), seniors are not as technophobic as they used to be. In fact, we are using smart phones, tablets, and e-readers in increasing numbers.

"Early adopters [of smart phones, tablets, and e-readers] tend to be younger and male. As consumer technology products gain wider acceptance, more women and more older consumers join the mix," says Don Kellogg, Director of Integrated Telecom Solutions at the Nielsen Company. "Tablets and e-readers are relatively easy to use. Couple that with light weight and the ability to increase the text size (not to be underestimated with older owners), and you have a very appealing product for older demographics," Kellogg said.[2]

Yet we hear more than a few ElderChicks continue to express fear and loathing when it comes to computer use, voicing lots of criticism of some of the gadgets, particularly smart phones, cell phones, and electronic game-playing devices. Let's listen in on a group of seniors discussing this in their condominium's community space:

- *I can't stand having to hear other people talking on their cell phones on the bus. There's no more eye contact with other people, just hearing what I don't wish to hear. There's so much less interaction possible.*

- *I've been to meetings where people who are supposed to be listening to each other are looking at their laps where they have their smart phones tuned in to something totally unrelated to what we're supposed to be dealing with!*

- *I've asked my daughter to please tell her children that they may not have electronic gadgets at the table when I'm there. Obviously, they allow it when I'm not.*

- *I'm not sure I welcome the feeling that I'm accessible (via e-mail, cell phone, etc.) twenty-four hours a day. I feel guilty when I ignore e-mail for a few days because I really want to feel totally private at times. Am I being rude?*

- *Now that I know my number appears at the other end when I make a call, I sometimes wonder whether the person not answering is just avoiding me. Is that paranoid?*

- *You have to be careful with e-mail! I've learned that it's easily misinterpreted. At least with voice mail your tone of voice conveys emotion, and of course with Skype you can see body language. We don't just communicate with our words.*

The free-wheeling discussion revealed that several people realized they were focusing on computer use as the source of much of what is wrong with today's world, all the way from the spread of terrorism, erosion of confidence in government, and all sorts of frightening fraudulent activities to bad manners, bad grammar, and evidence of deteriorating intelligence in younger generations. Peers suggested that they might try to focus not only on the many positive aspects of the enormous changes new technologies bring but also on the possibility that their own fear of change, of aging, or of feeling irrelevant is fueling their anger. Here are some comments of the computer defenders:

- *Computer technology has improved my health and longevity. I'm a cancer survivor, and I wouldn't be here today without it.*

- *Computers put global libraries into my home and my children's schools. When I want information about anything, it's at my fingertips. If I had to run to the library every time I wanted to know something, I wouldn't go and I wouldn't know.*

- *I don't have to travel to shop, bank, register to vote, renew my passport or my driver's license. I don't have to spend a lot of time on the phone on hold since I can do most stuff online.*

- *What about transportation? It's a lot safer to travel now, and I can get to a lot more places. Why would anyone want to go back to the old precomputer days?*

- *What motivated me to learn to use my computer is how close I can be to my kids and grandkids far away. They include me in their family texts about sports, we Skype, and we have weekly FaceTime sessions. I love that we take pictures with our iPhones and e-mail them on the spot. "Mom, do you like this sofa?" and "Look what Ben just did!" It's like we're not even apart.*

Detractors and defenders abound. Nevertheless, the fastest-growing demographic for Facebook and other social media are those people age fifty and over, according to the Pew Research Center's Internet & American Life Project.[3] Social networking use among Internet users ages fifty and older nearly doubled from 22 percent in April 2009 to 42 percent in May 2010, says a survey of more than 2,250 US adults. The figures were even higher for the oldest users: usage among those over the age of sixty-five percent grew 100 percent, from 13 percent in 2009 to 26 percent in May 2010.

Alice B is adapting to new technology rather easily:

I find e-reading easy on the eyes, both indoors and out. It's great on the beach, on a park bench, and in my living room. And when I'm traveling, it sure beats lugging around a bunch of novels and travel books. It's easy to hold and I can make the print any size I want with a flick of the finger. My iPhone also knows where I am on my e-reader and vice versa, so it's always ready in a traffic jam, when I'm early for an appointment, or when I have to wait for someone who isn't.

I was always one of those who just wanted a phone to allow me to hear and be heard by the person at the other end—which seemed be too much to ask of my old cell phone. But phones finally got really smart—or maybe I just decided to take the leap. Mine takes really good pictures. Okay, not museum quality, but certainly as good as my point-and-shoot camera—and I can keep them right on my phone and/or transfer them to my computer. Since it's always with me, I can record events on the spur of the moment. I also love having several Scrabble games on the go—with my friends as well as with my grandchildren across the country. My iPhone is also a GPS at my fingertips. When I'm walking (or driving), it knows where I am and helps me find whatever I'm looking for without having to ask someone.

Margaret F, a treasured ElderChick in England, not only adapted to using a computer, she took the adaptation an inspiring step further when Parkinson's disease got in the way:

Serendipitously, I was able to learn to use a computer when my husband was obliged to buy one to pursue his Open University course. I was delighted to realize that my touch-typing skills enabled me to send e-mails tripping off the key board with great spontaneity. Invaluable when two sons took off for the United States and Australia, and a wonderful way to keep in touch with friends abroad.

At last I was vindicated for canceling a postgraduate teacher training course in 1958 in favor of learning shorthand and typing. This move outraged my mother: she had been deprived of any real secondary education because her mother was a widow, so she was always determined that I should go as far as possible, thrilled when that took me to Oxford University, and outraged by a choice which she said "you could have done at sixteen." Perfectly true, and I did not escape doing the teacher training later (thus fulfilling the traditional destiny of the female graduate).

My husband prevented his brain from rusting in retirement by taking an Open University course and was rewarded for his tenacious effort with a first-class honors degree in mathematics. His graduation was a very Madden-proud day.

Nowadays, Parkinson's disease prevents me from touch typing, but I have installed Dragon, invaluable software for transferring voice to screen. Dragon and I have many hilarious tussles, but he is my lifeline to communication.

We're pleased to see that seniors are finally accepting some of the new gadgets. Of course, what is happening is not just gadgetry. Acceptance of new technology can be life changing in the way that telephones, television, and airplanes were for our parents and grandparents. But for those who want to take small steps into the twenty-first century, gadgets are a start.

We do know they're not for everyone, however. The dissenter-poet, **Lucia Blinn** of Chicago, Illinois, spoke to us in poetry:

Left Behind but Not Bereft

> You've no idea what a technophobe I am,
> *said my friend Pat, even as she in the next breath
> announced herself the new owner of an iPad2.
> So it's official: everyone's buying
> the next next thing, and I am not.
> Mired in a sleepy other time, I limp along
> with my not-very-smart phone,
> aging Mac Book and vintage Kindle.
> I will never be the one in a restaurant
> to look up the name of that actor in that movie
> we can't remember the title of.
> My phone will not take your picture
> or check the latest read-this-instant email.*

I cannot make a date with you unless I'm home
with my elderly fraying Filofax.
You have, the lot of you, left me behind
as you zoom into still another realm of thrilling,
life-changing, must-have stuff.
How disturbing is this to what passes
for my peace of mind?
How quickly can I finish this poem
and take a nap?

Phyllis R of Swarthmore, Pennsylvania, seems to agree with Lucia:

I'm even farther behind in the world of tech—I read books in paper and still read two newspapers every day. I carry my cell phone for emergency use, but I don't use it otherwise. I have a desktop iMac that is years behind the world, and I have a landline phone for all my calls. I don't have a CD player or an iPod. I don't have a digital camera. I am content in my low-tech life and wish it were possible to see anyone in a car who is not talking on a cell phone. I can look at the sky and enjoy the clouds and the sun, the full moon tonight, the sight of my grandchildren, and the company of my friends. Perhaps I live in a world of the past, but I don't miss what I never had.

Rita S of Beechwood, Ohio, has been a teacher all her adult life; she has taught in grade school, religious school, and university. When her children were young, she took a break from full-time teaching.

I was pregnant with my first child, and in those days, pregnant women were not allowed to teach. While I was raising my three kids, I worked part-time, did volunteer work, went to graduate school, and eventually received a doctorate. I've never really retired, although I'm many years past the usual age of retirement.

I taught at a small college for two years and then went on to a larger university, where I was department head and interim dean. I retired from that institution and became executive director of a nonprofit organization. But I'm a teacher to the core and continued to teach courses at the same time.

Then I took on a new kind of teaching. I was asked to teach a course online at a Cleveland university. E-learning teaching is really different from face-to-face teaching. I had to change the kinds of assignments and change the approach. There is no mutual immediate feedback between students and teacher. Since you don't see their faces, you don't know if they're actually getting it. There's no personal interaction with them, nor is there any interaction with each other. So I had to find ways to make them interact with each other, and the technology makes that harder to accomplish. I came kicking and screaming to the new technology. I preferred a no. 2 pencil and face-to-face teaching. But I learned what I had to learn because I had to do it in order to teach.

How can you possibly manage to maintain intimacy with your students? From planning, to delivery, to evaluation, and feedback, this has to be a huge change in every aspect of your pedagogical approach! Are you worried about whether they're "getting it?" How do you know they're actually learning?

That's a big problem that I wrestle with. One of the challenges is to make sure the courses are as rigorous as face-to-face teaching. Many students take online courses because they think they're easier. But that's not true for all. Unquestionably e-teaching serves a purpose. Some students were able to continue their academic programs while pregnant or tending small children at home. Some students live too far from the university or have no way to get there or don't feel safe traveling to night classes downtown. E-classes enable some students to work full time, which they may need to do if they are going to go to college at all.

Actually, there are advantages to e-teaching. I was able to in-corporate audiotapes, download live speeches, such as the president's speeches and Martin Luther King Jr.'s "I Have a Dream" speech. I can use source material from the Internet, and so much comes directly from the Internet. I can direct students to links to materials they never would have been able to access without this technology.

Rita is a shining example of someone who is continuing to learn despite getting older. So many in her age group believe that the Internet is a bad influence on society, and many seniors refuse to learn to use anything that smacks of computer technology. Like anything else, there is much good to be gained and much bad to be eschewed. It's all a matter of the use to which technological gadgets are put. That Rita has embraced the technology she needs to continue to teach is an inspiration—to other seniors and to the students who might otherwise have no access to a college education.

Julieta T-J has no intention of retiring from her position at a college in Philadelphia, Pennsylvania. In many ways, she has al-ready lived many lifetimes and has experienced many of the is-sues that the rest of the women in this book have, even though she is only fifty-seven. For her, every day is a preparation for what will come next.

When I was six years old, my mother left me with relatives in Panama and went to work as a domestic in a well-to-do family outside of Philadelphia. A year later, my mother sent for me, and I grew up in that home until my mother was able to buy a house of our own. I was treated as one of the family and went to excellent suburban schools. My mother raised me to have a wide worldview. She even managed on her modest salary to send me to Europe for three weeks when I finished high school.

Following high school, I attended Philadelphia Biblical University and then got my MS at Eastern University in nonprofit management. I am now on the faculty of the Community College of Philadelphia, as supervisor of the academic computer lab. I also teach courses in the Behavioral Health and Human Services Department.

I became a minister later in my adult life. I was ordained and became part of the ministerial staff of New Life Church of God. I minister monthly at the Self Help Movement Substance Abuse Services in Philadelphia.

What about your family, Julieta? With two simultaneous careers, I wonder what you are doing in your "other life."

On the way to this stage in my life, I have known separations and tragic losses. My first husband and I divorced, and I raised our two daughters alone. My older daughter is completing her degree in early childhood education. She has a learning disability, but not an intelligence deficit. She's very bright, and this difficulty has only made her more tenacious, struggling to complete one course at a time. She loves little kids and is so very sensitive to their needs because she has had so many learning needs of her own. My younger daughter worked with special-needs children as their advocate after she finished college and then went back to graduate school to get her MSW in social work. School is still very much on her mind as she is considering a PhD or law school.

Sometime after the divorce I married again but unfortunately spent four and a half of those five years of marriage caring for my husband when he became terminally ill as a result of exposure to Agent Orange. Our relationship was beautiful. Despite the pain and heartache of his illness, it was one of the most enriching times in my life. During that time, two baby nieces were orphaned, and my ill husband and I took them in, ultimately adopting them. They are fifteen and eighteen now and both wonderful and talented.

So now you have two teen-age daughters and two adult daughters. You're getting close to the next stage in your life. Do you have any new plans?

Not really. I'm just expecting to continue along the same vein. I have always thrown my hat into many rings and pursued many interests. I am always taking classes or starting a new enterprise. For a few years—for as long as the grant money held out—I worked every Saturday with high school students who were known to be at risk for dropping out of school. We realized that computer illiteracy was keeping them from competing with more fortunate kids who had computers at home or attended schools with good computer facilities. We found a great disparity in academic achievement between the kids who were computer literate and those who were computer illiterate. We called this the "digital divide," and we set out to bridge it. Today most schools are better equipped to prepare kids technologically.

And now I see a new digital divide. Many seniors are helpless in front of a computer. They can send e-mails and maybe buy things online, but that is often the extent of it. They are kind of out of it when it comes to getting new information or staying in touch with a lot of what's going on in the world. They're being left behind. And the digital divide will widen the older they get. I hate to think of all those people who will become set apart from so many in society because they are unwilling to learn and unable to use new technology.

Julieta, why is learning all this worth the trouble?

Even looking up a phone number is now an online skill, since telephone directories are no longer delivered to each house. Think what an advantage it is to be able to bank online. Solving many issues can be done online—without all that waiting time on telephone hold if you know how to do your requesting and complaining online. Also, older people who become less mobile can be so much more in this world if they have devel-

oped computer skills. Computer skills are now expected, and people don't realize how much easier it is to navigate their lives if they have opened their minds to the possibilities of the computer.

When I reflect on my life, I regard every day as a possibility for a new stage of development in my future. I don't know what the next step will be or what the next stage will bring, but I feel I'm prepared for it. (Oh! I'm going to spend time with a family in Peru in May. The language department at my college offered this as professional development. I'm always up for that, and they even gave me a grant to cover part of the cost.)

What an inspiration Julieta is! No (worthwhile) job or challenge is too big or too small to win her attention. She's at mid-life, with the expectation that the future holds as much promise, abundance, and vibrancy as the past. And she's passing that spirit on to her students and her own kids.

BEYOND THE GADGETS

Take heart, technophobes! Keeping up with the new gadgets, we found, is not the only way for ElderChicks to remain in touch with the contemporary world.

There are many other avenues for learning that not only keep our minds active but keep us emotionally healthy and growing as we age. For instance, brain studies have shown the particularly salutary effects of learning to play an instrument or study a foreign language long past the stage in life when someone else was there to make us practice. Exploring new areas of interest and new ways of expressing ourselves or reconnecting with old interests is not busywork but a positive step in a new direction. For some, teaching or applying what we know in new contexts expands our horizons.

We discovered how that is working for shining examples of ElderChicks who have left earlier careers:

> **Elena S**: *I have actually been thinking more and more about our universe. I find, now that I am seventy-five, I am becoming more interested in dark matter, time bending, black holes, quantum physics, alternate universes. It's like there is some energy out there that is pulling me in, and I'm amazed every time I find a new bit of information.*
>
> *I feel that we are living in a big magic box, and each time I hear of a new discovery or dimension, my eyes and my mind pop with excitement.*
>
> *Is my new curiosity due to the fact that I am at the last quarter of my life on earth and am feeling the gravitational pull from some place "out there?"*

We interviewed **Mary Catherine D**, who directs a senior center in Havertown, Pennsylvania, that offers well-attended classes in the arts. She sees people with no previous experience as artists finding new avenues of expression and emotional release. Mary Catherine sees people break through an initial "But I can't draw!" reluctance to reach appreciation of the process involved in making art as opposed to expecting perfection in the product. She posits a direct line between tapping into creativity to the resilience that healthy aging demands.

Tamah G of Rockville, Maryland, retired from her school librarian and media specialist career, consciously planned for the role of art in her retirement:

> *Although I have been working in glass and as a glass artist for over thirty years, it became even more important to me as I approached retirement. Knowing that I would have more time to find ways to try new techniques, to improve on the ones I already have, to take classes that appeal to me was an impor-*

tant part of my retirement planning. My vocation was among books. My avocation was and is working to create something with my hands.

Like anything else, the first times I worked in glass, the results were, to say the least, not all that appealing to anyone. Except to me. I had created something. With my hands. It was visible and tangible. The feeling one gets at the end of the creative process is not only relief but amazement. And often, but not always, satisfaction. Of course, there are many times when a piece will not look good, or when, in my case, something explodes in the kiln or breaks when I am taking it somewhere.

Drawing and painting, it seems to me, are more forgiving. If it doesn't work out, it's less painful and far less expensive to abandon the piece. But even if you or I am not going to be the next . . . (fill in the blank with the name of a great artist in whatever field you attempt), working at it takes you away from where you are. My mother used to tell me that when she went to the studio to work on a clay sculpture, even when she was feeling low or harried or stressed, the minute she began to work on the clay with her hands, the tension fell away. And so it is. The focus on the process is in another world.

The creative process gives satisfaction. Visual art, sculpture, cooking, baking, gardening, and more. They bring results that give a feeling of accomplishment, satisfaction, and that bring an enormous amount of pleasure to yourself and to others.

Marilyn Arnold of Kansas City, Missouri, learned to sew as a child and in 4-H as a young Missourian. After a career as an insurance executive, she started Marilyn Arnold Designs:

My mind is awhirl now with all of the ideas I have in starting a new business. As my friend, Pat, says, "I am beginning my second act." A number of years ago I had a wonderful friend, Millie. Millie was in her eighties at the time and was one of the happiest, most content women I have seen. Her secret was to

accept each stage in life and make the most of it. I have strived
to live by that for the last twenty years.

Now I am following my passion by starting my own business
after navigating the corporate world for twenty-nine years! I
am making pillows from wedding dresses. I take someone's
dress that has been hanging in their closet for ten, twenty,
thirty, forty years and turn it into a beautiful pillow that they
can give to a daughter, granddaughter, niece or keep for them-
selves. My customers have tears in their eyes when they see
what I have created.

Marilyn has found that her new learning and new business bring
satisfaction in unexpected ways. Seeing the pleasure her work
brings her customers is what a professor of ours used to call
"psychic income."

Georgia B of Blue Bell, Pennsylvania, earns psychic income
through her love of animals. We found that Georgia was tapping
into her great feeling for dogs—and humans—to expand her
knowledge of both in a way that benefits all three, the dog, people
who need emotional support, and herself. We asked her to tell us
about it:

I have always loved dogs. Even though he bit me when I tried
to remove chewing gum from his mouth, I still loved my first
dog, Slim. Chico, a mixed breed from the pound, used to sit on
my bed and sing "Cross over the Bridge," which in retrospect
was probably quite a bit of annoying howling. At age eight I
didn't think so at all. After a long career in education that
included teaching, administration, and consulting, I retired
(almost), and I finally get to spend time with my dog again.
This time my best friend's name is Tali . . . short for Natalia,
then Talia, and finally, when she did not respond to either of
those, Tali.

We work together, Tali and I, doing what is called pet therapy. We are a team, certified by the Delta Society, a national organization that sponsors and insures pet partners throughout the country. We passed a rather rigorous exam and work hard to get recertified every two years.

Tell me a little about pet therapy. Where do you do this and what do you actually do?

We work in libraries in the Doggie Tales program, where I get to listen to young children read. Tali listens too, placing her head on a child's lap, and provides two large, nonjudgmental ears. We are also involved in a program for seventh-grade "struggling" readers. Tali doesn't know this, and she treats these boys and girls with the same respect as the superstars in the "Bluebird" group. We visit hospitals, where I get to meet some very interesting folks, and Tali provides the tactile therapy that calms these often anxious patients.

Recently we were involved in a wellness program in a life-care community. As Tali and I grow older together, we visit residents who grow older with us, moving from independent living to assisted living and, finally, to skilled nursing. We have said goodbye to quite a few friends, and even though I am sad to see them die, I know that our visits were meaningful to them and that my dog helped to enrich their lives at the end of their days. There is little to compare with the glimmer in the eyes of an Alzheimer's patient as she pets Tali or the determination of someone suffering from Parkinson's disease when his hand stops shaking as it works its way through Tali's thick fur.

Although I suspect that spending time with me is enough fun for my dog, we do have special outings as well. My husband, Syl, and I take her to the beach here in Venice, Florida, and she swims in the Gulf of Mexico. Most borzois, I'm told, do not like the water, but Tali is very fond of it.

Although I am very active in my retirement, exercising every day, playing bridge with other couples, chairing adult educa-

tion at our local Jewish center, painting large canvases and furniture, singing in the choir, teaching Sunday School, and, yes, still lecturing for the Bureau of Education and Research, the most important part of my retirement is spending time with my dog. My elder years have been enriched by this wonderful animal, and I am very grateful to be able to grow old with her.

After her beloved Tali died at a good age, Georgia waited a short while before she adopted two more dogs and trained them as pet therapy animals as well. One of her first outings with them was to a residential care facility shortly after Hurricane Sandy. Georgia tells us that the combination of the storm and her visit provided new insight:

Hurricane Sandy has reminded us all about the power of nature. How we respond to losing electrical power challenges our ability to adapt. Candles, flashlights, bottled water, extra food . . . these are the immediate essentials that we gather. Living without our beloved devices that depend on electricity takes a bit more inner strength. But what about the loss of "power" as we age? Today, I visited an elderly woman, age ninety-three, in a home where she will live for the rest of her life. I visited her with my pet therapy dogs, Gianni and Dante, hoping to bring a bit of joy into her dreary day.

After hearing the well-worn anecdotes about her beloved pup, we engaged in a more serious discussion. She is reluctant to share her thoughts with her children as she does not want them to feel guilty for placing her in an "institution," her term, not mine. She does not want to complain to those who take care of her as she does not want to be known as a "kvetch," again, her word. She feels powerless. She cannot take care of her basic needs. She cannot choose her food or when to bathe. She cannot choose her friends as most of the residents do not know that they are even there. The only power she has is in her motorized wheelchair in which she rolls down the endless corridors. How does one adapt to this loss of control? How does one meet these challenges? She is powerless . . . not because the lights went out after a loss of electricity but because the light has been extinguished in her soul. As my dogs licked her frail hand, I think I noticed a spark, a slight flicker in her eyes.

Sharon B of Longboat Key, Florida, whom you will hear from again in future chapters, said that she is always a student of what she doesn't know how to do or know how to do well enough. She sets a high bar for herself. As we were speaking, Sharon had a camera with a very, very long lens hanging around her neck. At the conclusion of our conversation, she was off to a private photography lesson.

> *I've always been interested in a lot of things. I've done photography since I was a child. Since photography has changed so significantly over the years I have had to upgrade my skill level and my knowledge.*
>
> *I don't know a lot of things, and there is so much to learn. I'm desperate to know more. I'm never short of material to explore. And there's almost nothing that doesn't interest me. So my curiosity is never satisfied. I guess I'm lucky; I don't need to push myself to learn new skills. Sometimes it seems there's just not enough time.*

The people we've met in this chapter embrace new learning. Whatever the impetus—to adapt to the techno-world around us, to express emotions or ideas in unfamiliar ways, to explore interests they never had time for when they were younger, or to apply professional expertise in new contexts—they shine from within.

New learning begets new energy. New learning sharpens the mind. New learning means growth. Many women told us they can't wait for the days that they attend classes. They have said they wished they had put as much effort and time into school when they were kids as they do now. They find themselves committed to learning in a new way—because they are genuinely curious, not because it is a "required course." Their priorities, of course, may have been different when they were much younger, and the excitement of learning was much less compelling than the excitement of pleasing their peers. Too bad, but not too late!

Sometimes it takes a cattle prod to find the right class to attend, the best hobby to pursue, or your way into cyberspace. The temptation to put off the search until tomorrow or let something else interfere is too appealing. It is difficult to resist the inertia that attends the easy life in retirement. But if you allow that inertia to set in, before you know it, the monotony of your life will hold less meaning and more boredom. The slope to irrelevance is downward and swift. Don't let this happen to you!

What are you learning?

7

WE LAUGH ABOUT OUR "SENIOR MOMENTS"

Should We Fear Them?

Memory is a complicated thing, a relative to truth, but not its twin.

—Barbara Kingsolver

- Ever stop to think and forget to start again?
- When I told the doctor about my memory loss, he made me pay in advance.
- Of all the things I've lost, I miss my mind the most.
- Seen it all, done it all. Can't remember most of it.
- Who are these kids and why are they calling me Mom?

Fear of losing our memory is fertile ground for dark humor. Humor masks our fears in the same way that whistling in the dark does. We laugh about what scares us because it feels a whole lot better than worrying about it. We know that laughter doesn't make fear go away, but neither does obsessing over what we may not be able to change.

Are forgetfulness and declining intellect inevitable? Is there anything we can do about it? In this chapter, we'll report what women have said about memory issues and also what medical research has to say about it.

Jane D of Wilmington, Delaware, is eighty-six years old and the oldest player in her tennis group. Yet she is the one who remembers the score most accurately. Jane is proactive: her techniques are *focus*, *intention*, and *seeking alternatives*.

> *I occasionally have trouble retrieving a word, but if I wait a few seconds, it usually turns up. If not, I go through the alphabet until I reach a letter that triggers what I'm looking for. If I find it—great! If not, I don't berate myself or my memory. There are plenty of other good words I can use.*

> *If you make it a point to* intend *to remember, you will have a much better chance of remembering. If you intend to forget, you probably will. So it's important to eliminate negative expectations. I also work on* focusing *my attention. Most of the time, it's not that we forget it. We just don't "get it" in the first place because we're not paying attention.*

Debra S of Tom's River, New Jersey, believes that active creativity is an essential factor in keeping the cobwebs out of her mind. She meets regularly with other artists where they spur each other's drive to remain current and committed to lively participation in the world.

> *I will be eighty-five next April, and I am one of the youngest in my poetry group. Most of the members are former teachers, testimony to the mindset about getting better with age. I have always believed that attitude colors our lives . . . and so I am a cockeyed optimist, perhaps a bit too "ballsy" for an "antique," but what the heck, I always leave my audience laughing. And I'm never timid about pushing my agenda.*

Joan S of Philadelphia, Pennsylvania, is comforted by the fact that she never could remember appointments. Since this is not a new problem—not the result of the aging process—she doesn't let it worry her. Joan thinks we sometimes beat ourselves up over this when we shouldn't. Perhaps we forget that we always had lapses of memory but didn't just attribute them to age. We love Joan's spirit!

> Some of the things we forget we have always forgotten, so don't forget that and take heart. No question that my memory is not as good as it should be. We all worry about it, and some of us for good reason, but it doesn't mean that we have Alzheimer's. For some of us it just means leaving more notes on the kitchen table. We have to pause and think—and it eventually comes back.
>
> I will be eighty-two next week, and damned if I look it or act it or feel it. I'm one of the lucky ones who is very healthy and active. I volunteer, I take art classes, I belong to a book club, and I still do freelance writing for former clients of my public relations firm. I don't play mah jong or cards—those aren't the friends I really want at this point. I want people who are alive and aware and active. Eighty is definitely the new sixty. Eighty-two is pretty good also.

The issue of memory inevitably comes up at almost all of our Lunch and Listen workshops.

Esther R of Monroe Township, New Jersey:

> When I hear or read an interesting lecture or essay, I know that I'm not going to remember all the details. So I make a special effort to absorb the whole idea and not beat myself up for not remembering all the details. I think a major component is intention. I may not remember what I had for lunch yesterday. But when I go into a roomful of people, and if the people are important to me, I will make it my business to remember

everybody's name. It takes more effort, it takes more will than it used to. But I like people and I'm willing to make the effort. Because it is important to me, I will do it.

We also asked women about their earlier memories. We wondered whether they deliberately try to retrieve earlier ones. Do they like to live in the past? Prefer to focus on the future?

Esther G of Milwaukee, Wisconsin:

My mother had beautiful penmanship and also wrote well creatively. My daughters bought her a book and asked her to write about her life. She started to do it and then we heard no more about it. When I asked her how the writing was coming along, she said to me, "I got to a certain point and then stopped. I realized that I don't want to do this. I don't want to think about those things—even the good ones." At ninety, she consciously decided that looking back was not something she enjoyed. She was happy, she said, in the present. I once asked her if she worried about the future, and she told me, "No, there isn't any." I know she didn't feel that way when she was younger!

Elena S of Monroe Township, New Jersey:

I have very few memories of my early life. I've sort of worried about that. Why don't I remember? I don't seem to have any recollection of a life before I was ten years old! I don't think it was because I was living in another language then. But that might be it. I was born in Cuba and just remember the last place where we lived. There was no trauma that I'm aware of. My family was a normal family. I wish I could remember. It's a whole chunk of my life that's missing.

Joan A of Haddonfield, New Jersey:

I find that lately early memories are flooding into my mind. I find it amazing that my children, my friends, my relatives, and

I have vastly differing memories of the same event! How can this be? Some of my most cherished and treasured memories have been absolutely denied by others. Especially my children. Memories that warm the wee wakeful hours of my insomniac nights never happened as far as my kids are concerned. How could they have forgotten? Have I remembered it wrong? Have they?

How does the mind manage to con us into such certainty about our perceptions—different for each person? We are all adamant that ours is the correct version. We also know that none of us lies. Are our memories diluted and polluted when they enter the cauldron of our mind? Do we adjust our memories to protect us from behaviors or feelings we would rather forget? Do we embroider memories to enhance our feeling of well-being? How much of our past history is a fairy tale we tell ourselves?

Nancy M of Haddonfield, New Jersey:

I do find myself focusing on the past, but not as a way to call up old times, necessarily. Sometimes I find myself focusing on what I did wrong or what I might hve done differently. It's a waste of time to obsess about a situation that can't be changed, such as having guilt about someone who has died. But I feel I can gain if I use that obsessing on the past as a way to change future behavior.

Cynthia G of Melrose Park, New Jersey:

I'm trying to reach a point where I can calmly reflect on things that happened or I still might feel guilty about. I definitely know in my head that I can't change the past anyway, and I guess I have to forgive myself in my heart. As a Catholic, sometimes I can even feel guilty when I realize that I shouldn't be harboring feelings of guilt when I know I've confessed and been forgiven. Maybe [laughing] memory loss wouldn't be so bad!

Nancy:

> *There's a big difference between forgetting and letting go, isn't there!*

Yes, memory is of great concern to us now.

- Will my memory fail me?

- Did the things I remember really happen the way I think they did?

- Can I do anything about preserving my memory?

FACTS AND MYTHS ABOUT MEMORY

What are the facts and myths of memory function as we age? First, we are wrong to regard memory as a singular entity. Or a single enemy, for that matter. Here's why.

Memory is often broken down into two types: short-term and long-term. Short-term memory, which is sometimes called your working memory, stores information that you need to remember in the immediate seconds, minutes, or hours. An example would be a telephone message that you are given and must remember until you pass it on. Long-term memory stores information that your brain retains because it is important to you. Basic information remembered includes names of family and friends, your address, and information on how to do certain activities and ordinary tasks. Long-term memory can be further divided into explicit, implicit, and semantic memory:

- *Explicit memories* are facts that you made a conscious effort to learn and that you can remember at will, for example, the names of state capitals.

- *Implicit memory* is information you draw on automatically in order to perform actions, such as driving to a familiar place or dialing an often-used phone number.

- *Semantic memories* are facts that are so deeply ingrained that they require no effort to recall. An example would be the days of the week.

It is important to realize that age-related memory loss sometimes occurs with explicit memory, but age has little or no effect on implicit or semantic memory.

Do memory-enhancing strategies help?

Several scientific studies[1] have reported that many older adults believe that although aging impairs memory, there is much they can do to help themselves offset the negative impact of age on memory. The good news is that their views are borne out by research which concludes that although aging does often negatively affect memory, certain strategies and lifestyle choices can have a beneficial impact on memory function.[2] In these studies, individual use (or nonuse) of memory-enhancing techniques did appear to influence older adults' ability to recall. This reinforces the argument that training older persons in certain strategic behaviors may be important for enhancing memory function in everyday life. We are not here to tell you what strategies to try. You'll have to do your own research for that, and it's worth the effort.

What about food?

There is further evidence that higher blood levels of omega-3 fatty acids and vitamins B, C, D, and E are associated with better mental functioning in the elderly. The average age in this study[3] was eighty-seven! Research results indicated that people with the highest blood levels of these four vitamins scored higher on six commonly used cognitive tests of mental functioning and had larger brain volume than those with the lowest levels. Higher blood levels of transfats, on the other hand, were significantly associated with impaired mental ability and smaller brain volume.

The lead author, Gene L. Bowman, a researcher in neurology at Oregon Health and Science University, said that the study could not determine whether taking supplements of these nutrients would actually decrease the risk for dementia. "But," he said, "What's the harm in eating healthier? Fish, fruits, vegetables all have these nutrients, and staying away from transfats is one key thing you can do."

The bottom line is that there's good news and bad news.

The bad news is that our memory function may indeed diminish as we age. The good news is that we may be able to use more deliberate techniques such as mnemonics, note taking, and other means to ensure successful remembering. In fact, doing so could lead to functional memory performance that is equivalent to our younger minds despite age changes in our cognition.

Of course, the elephant in the room—every time we have a "senior moment"— is the nagging thought: Is it Alzheimer's, or just a memory slip? Everyone has moments of forgetfulness— misplaced keys, a forgotten errand, the name of that book you just read and loved but can't get off the tip of your tongue. Just how serious are these slips? We suggest you read the Harvard Medical School Special Health Report *A Guide to Alzheimer's Disease* to get a clearer sense of normal versus worrisome forgetfulness.

AND NOW A WORD ABOUT HERBAL REMEDIES FOR MEMORY DEFICITS

In the United States, herbal remedies have been labeled "alternative"—this means that most are not considered to be a part of accepted medical practice—for a variety of reasons:

- *Scientific Testing:* It is difficult to scientifically test herbal therapies in the same way that prescription drugs are tested. The conventional medical community relies on scientific evidence when evaluating the safety and effectiveness of alternative therapies. So far, very little research has been devoted to testing herbal and other alternative therapies.

- *Medical Education*: Many non-Western healing practices are not taught in United States medical schools. Many board-certified physicians have not studied alternative medicine. It's up to you to ask.

- *Medical Insurance*: Many alternative therapies and supplements are not available to patients in US hospitals unless they are covered by health insurance. Most are not covered.

- *Proof of Safety*: Unlike companies that produce drugs (which must be tested before being sold), the companies that make herbal and diet supplements are not required to prove to the Food and Drug Administration (FDA) that their supplements are safe or effective. However, they must not claim the supplements can prevent, treat, or cure any specific disease. Read the labels carefully!

- *Quality Control*: Some of the products may not contain the amount of the herb or substance that is on the label, and some may include other substances (contaminants). Actual amounts per dose may vary between brands or even between different batches of the same brand. Remember, quality control is voluntary by the manufacturer, not by an impartial agency as FDA approved drugs are. In 2007, the FDA wrote new rules to improve the quality of manufacturing for dietary supplements and the proper listing of supplement ingredients. But it's important to understand that these rules do not address the safety of the ingredients or their effects on health.

- ***Interactions***: Most such supplements have not been tested to find out whether they interact with medicines, foods, or other herbs and supplements. Even though some reports of interactions and harmful effects may be published, full studies of interactions and effects are not often available. Because of these limitations, any information on ill effects and interactions should be considered incomplete.

Simply put, you cannot buy herbal remedies with complete confidence. You should be aware of the caveats when you use them.

If you do decide to go with herbal remedies for memory enhancement, do your research. When you search the Internet for anything, get to know the difference between websites whose URLs end in

.com

.gov

.edu

.org

- website addresses that end with *.com.* or *.net* are usually sponsored by companies or people who are trying to sell you a product or an idea. The "research" they quote may be paid for by manufacturers who naturally want to sell you their products.

- Websites of government-sponsored research from such sources as the National Institutes of Health (NIH) or the Centers for Disease Control (CDC) will end in *.gov*.

- University research and medical center websites will end in *.edu*. Government and university websites are not trying to sell you products.

- Websites of nonprofit organizations will end in *.org*. Be sure to check out the goals and purpose of the organization.

Here are some websites that are all available free of charge, without subscription:

- FDA Center for Food Safety and Applied Nutrition: Dietary Supplements:http://www.fda.gov/food/dietarysupplements/default.htm .

- National Center for Complementary and Alternative Medicine (NCCAM):http://nccam.nih.gov/.

- NIH Office of Dietary Supplements (ODS) http://ods.od.nih.gov/

WHAT DOES ALL THIS MEAN FOR US AS WE AGE?

It means there is no room for mental laziness. There are many resources out there for help with some of these memory-enhancing strategies. Some of these resources are suggested in the endnotes to this chapter, and we urge you to try some of them with all the persistence of your younger years. It always took work to live well and we mustn't stop now! Just as we exercise our bodies with as much vigor as we can muster to stay as fit as we can, so must we continue to exercise our minds with fresh ideas, new skills, and known memory-enhancing strategies.

Though we expect to lose some physical stamina and abilities, let's not roll over and play dead until we are.

8

RX HEALTH

We Can't Ignore the Changes. What Do We Do about Them?

A healthy attitude is contagious but don't wait to catch it from others. Be a carrier.

—Tom Stoppard

SO HOW ARE YOU?

Such an innocent question! What does it mean when you hear it or ask it? And how much do you really want to know? How long is your answer? Does it depend on who's listening? Do you tell only close friends or family, or do visits with friends become "organ recitals?"

Our health becomes a prime concern as we begin to notice aches and pains that we never had before; for some of us it becomes the major focus of our lives: what your doctor said, what's wrong with anyone we know, when we had what you have, what my doctor said, and on and on. Others of us seem to carry on with our lives despite critical health issues and manage to maintain our attention to the world beyond ourselves.

Proposed changes in health care are happening quickly, and just at the time that statistics tell us we are beginning to need it most. Some physicians are switching to "boutique" practices, leaving their patients having to find new doctors. Some of us find ourselves without sufficient health care. Some of us are burdened with our children's health care because they aren't covered. Will the care that we expected for ourselves be available to us? This is worrisome. Health issues appear to consume so much more of the time and concern of people reaching retirement and beyond.

For some seniors, as they begin to notice aches and pains they never had before, health becomes the major focus of their lives, while others seem to carry on despite critical health issues, managing to maintain attention to the world beyond themselves even as they endure difficult treatments. Some become absorbed in the physical condition of their relatives and friends to the degree that other people's symptoms become their own, like the "sympathy pains" some fathers may suffer during pregnancy and childbirth.

What is so different for us today? For one thing, we are bombarded with the commercials telling us what to tell our doctors! Not only are we urged to request drugs we never heard of before, but some of the drugs are for ailments we never heard of either. (When did our legs become "restless"?) So while we gratefully celebrate medical advances and technology that are helping us live longer, some among us are starting to feel overwhelmed.

TAKING CHARGE AND BEING RESPONSIBLE FOR OUR HEALTH

Some of us are fortunate to have another person, relative or friend, to accompany us to doctors' appointments. These are occasions, when we actually have health problems, when two heads and four ears really are better than one. Someone taking notes can be an advantage, especially when emotions are running high and may obscure memory or attention. When their mother first was diagnosed with cancer in her late '60's, **Patricia d R's** children leapt into action. Her daughter, **Andrea K**, of Haddonfield, New Jersey, was closest on the scene, but Andrea's brothers flew in from Mexico or drove in from Washington whenever they could. Andrea's account tells the story:

It was September 2005 when my mother was diagnosed with cancer on the base of her tongue. It was Labor Day 2005, to be exact. We got the call confirming what we hoped wasn't true, that the biopsy was cancer, squamous cell carcinoma. And like that, in an instant, we were all flung into the world of cancer. Any of you who have been there, or are there, know what I am talking about. Suddenly you have immediate appointments with several doctors who recommend several scans. This insane whirlwind led me to make the first of two binders for my mom during her battle with cancer.

At our first appointment with the surgical oncologist I realized we were about to get a bomb of information dropped on us: blood results, scan results, doctors' numbers, emergency doctors' numbers, pamphlets on cancer, side effects, depression, nausea. I get nauseated just thinking about it all! At the time, I realized that we needed to take care of all of this information, mainly her appointments, doctors' numbers, medication lists, scan results, and blood counts. I could tell that my mom and dad were too overwhelmed to keep track of it all, so I created a binder that would hold all these documents. This medical binder ended up helping us all. I remember a frantic search through the binder when I needed a doctor's number when my mother was too wiped out to direct me. The binder went with my mom to all her appointments. When friends helped out by taking her to appointments, they were able to find information for the doctors. I still have the binder somewhere, a history of rough times past.

After one of our first appointments with my mother's radiation oncologist, the other binder was born. My mother, father, and I met with him about a week after her diagnosis. It seemed like we were in his office for hours. He spent a very long time describing all the things that were going to happen to her because of the radiation to her neck: redness, sores in her mouth, muscle damage, thick saliva. The list went on and on, and he didn't hold back. When he left the room, my mom and I looked at each other and wondered out loud, "Who in their right mind would go through with this?" Of course, we both knew the answer, a lot of people like my mom had a lot of reasons to live.

That night I went home and started working on the "Reasons to Keep Going" book. This is part of a letter I wrote to my mom and put in on the first page of the book: "We wondered who would willingly go through with everything that he said would happen to you. I know that some days we will wonder why we should keep going, so I put together this book to remind us why. Mainly to remind you why you should keep going. I know you know why you are proceeding bravely though all this torture, but I thought it might help to remind you how important you are to me and everyone that knows you.

For every week of treatment I will add to this book, and I hope that in some way it will help you through this hard time we are passing through. I believe, I know, it is temporary and in a couple of months you will be yourself again and we will all rejoice and celebrate together. It will be a BIG celebration." I added to the book weekly, and her friends sent in pictures, poems, notes. It is a beautiful collection of photos and goals for when treatment ended and she got better.

My beloved mom died December 26, 2010. But she did get better for a while, and during that time we did some big living and checked off some of those dreams we had collected in the book for when she was better. I will carry those memories with me forever.

Patricia's attitude and courage and her family's devotion and care were admired by everyone who knew them—from home to hospital to hospice experiences. They inspired each other as they somehow found the spirit and love to keep each other going. They accepted the limits of what medical science could provide and also accepted the responsibility for whatever they could do, and they did it with creativity and determination. As we said in chapter 1:

The science of mastering this stage in our lives is up to our doctors. The art is up to us.

WHAT ARE PRACTICAL THINGS WE CAN DO?

We talked to **Dr. Don Friedman**, the retired head of rheumatology at Crozier-Chester Hospital in Chester, Pennsylvania, who teaches medical students about ethics and how to relate to patients respectfully and humanely. He also advises older patients as a practical health care advisor. He gave us lots of practical advice:

- Find the right doctor.
- Is your doctor someone you can comfortably relate to?
- Is your doctor willing to listen? If not, find another.
- Get references.
- Interview your doctor.

On this topic, the experience of **Jean A of Philadelphia, Pennsylvania**, can be a lesson for us all. After a radical hysterectomy, necessitated by endometrial cancer, her surgeon's remark, "I know what you're going through," as he removed many, many staples from her body did not convince her, considering he was in his forties and had endured only an appendectomy in his much younger life. Jean found both his and his nurse's attitudes patronizing and even demeaning. And being a well-informed patient who had learned all she could about her postoperative treatment, she also questioned its validity. Taking matters into her own hands, Jean found the well-published head of the relevant department at an associated hospital and asked for an appointment. There she met the surgeon, who was frank ("The prognosis is not good"), understanding ("Be sure to get an iPod so you can be distracted pleasantly during long, boring treatment sessions"), ready to change the program she found questionable, and respectful of her request to interview him before asking him to take the case, which he did. The happy news is that she survived years beyond the surgery and remains appreciative of what she found to be a mutually satisfying doctor-patient relationship.

Dr. Friedman emphasizes the many ways we can help ourselves in optimizing visits with doctors and managing our own illnesses. To make the most of a visit to the doctor:

- Make a list of the questions you need to ask and the information you need to share.

- Ask what the information you're given means; lab results, suggestions for lifestyle changes, and so on.

- Be sure you understand the instructions you are given and your responsibilities for managing your treatment. Repeat them back to your doctor to be sure you've interpreted them correctly.

We can improve our health, according to Dr. Friedman, by examining our own emotional reactions, by recognizing our own spiritual resources, and by recognizing the activities that bring us comfort and a feeling of well-being. Walking, reading, communicating with family or friends, listening to music, and meditating have real and positive effects on health. What good advice, Dr. Friedman. We're listening.

BE YOUR OWN RESEARCH ASSISTANT

On your own, learn all you can about your illness, follow instructions, and be open to discussing the way your illness affects you emotionally with your doctor, family, or friends.

Take advantage of the Internet and all the helpful information it has to offer. But know that there's a lot of junk out there –misinformation from people who are trying to sell you stuff or tell you things that have no basis in fact. Please refer back to chapter 7 where we discussed the differences among websites that end in

.com: websites that want to sell you a product or an idea

.org: websites that represent a group. *Be sure to check out the group!*

.edu: websites that represent a college, university, or medical center

.gov: websites that are sponsored by the United States government

Medical reports and newsletters from highly respected medical centers can be an excellent source of supplementary information.

You may recall meeting Jean A earlier—in chapter 3. Her early experiences and lifelong interest in archaeology and anthropology have served her well in making decisions about avoiding unnecessary surgery in another situation. Just after buying a Razor scooter to use around her neighborhood, Jean was off to Turkey, where she broke her ankle badly. She could understand and accept the need for surgery when she got home (and gave the Razor scooter to a happy teenage neighbor), but her background in archaeology led her to say no to hip replacement surgery later on. Having unearthed, examined, and reconstructed some thirteen skeletons in one summer's training in the archaeological field school, Jean looked at her own x-rays and decided there was still some room between the bones and that she'd rather rely on aspirin and Tylenol and manage with a cane when necessary. And so she does.

We are fortunate to live in a country where excellent health care is available. Doctors are well trained and hospitals are equipped with state-of-the-art tools. However, doctors are not gods, but are very human and very busy, and there are lots of them. If a doctor is too busy to answer your questions or isn't respectful of your need to understand, it might be in your best interest to find another doctor. Also, being human, doctors do make mistakes, and patients must be intelligent consumers by being proactive and becoming as informed as possible. There are often more options available than you think, and you should try to be aware of them. Get a second opinion. Check out reliable sources. We're not talking colds and flu here. We're talking serious illness.

Sharon B, whom you have already met and will hear from again in chapter 9, never lets an opportunity to improve a situation pass her by. In this case, it was a health situation.

> *My husband has Parkinson's disease. About two and a half years ago, while watching PBS on television, I learned about the Mark Morris Dance Group at the Brooklyn Academy of Music, which had developed a program called Dance for Parkinson's. While in New York, I went to a Mark Morris dance performance. Because I had a knee injury at the time, I took the elevator and was joined by many people with walkers, canes, and various walking aids. I asked them if they knew about Dance for Parkinson's classes. Not only did they know about it, but they told me how much it meant to them to participate with their spouses in this group.*

The Mark Morris Dance Group trains teachers from all over the world for these classes, which are held weekly for people who have Parkinson's and their caregivers. I became very interested and contacted the director about starting a group in Sarasota. He and I have developed a relationship over these years. I sent my husband's caregiver to New York to be trained, and I went to Gainesville, Florida, for training. I'm not a dancer, so I'm not going to be leading any classes. But I wanted to learn firsthand what they were about.

There are many dimensions to this, many reasons why these classes are so valuable. One is the physical movement. Parkinson's is a condition of restricted movement, and these dances are designed to help people move better. Another dimension is social. Most Parkinson's patients become isolated. Here they meet, dance, and support each other. The class has become a community that cares about each other. They go to class, then out to lunch. When someone can't come, they call to let the others know why. Participation in the group has become more than a morning's activity; it has generated a community. A third dimension is that it's simply fun. And most Parkinson's patients don't have much fun. The classes enable people with limitations to do something rather than sit around and feel sorry for themselves.

The lesson here is not just what can be done for Parkinson's, but how Sharon's story can be applied to many of the other health situations that may occur in our lives past sixty. We have to take charge and be very proactive and extremely creative about improving situations. Sharon happened to be watching TV, was impressed by what she saw, and contacted the guy in charge. Together they made something wonderful happen. Sharon doesn't sit around and say "Someone ought to do something about this." She knows that *she* can be the someone.

Pat W, a blogger, reported this:

I did something yesterday that I'm very proud of. When I turned sixty-five this year, I took Healthnet as my Medicare provider. A month later I received a card called the Silver Sneakers card. It said it was a free membership to a health club/gym. Free was the operative word. I didn't believe it, but I kept the card.

I'm a little chubby and have terrible joint pain as a result of experimental stage 3B melanoma treatment six years ago. At the time, they gave me three to seven months to live. Old story—that was six years ago. But it did leave me with terrible joint pain, so I've lost all my muscle tone.

Yesterday I decided that it wasn't going to get any better on its own. So I went to this gym—lovely place—they have Senior Silver Sneakers classes at several levels. A ladies' exercise room, a pool, a sauna, a spa, back and abs room, weight room, and the list goes on and on. I really thought they would say, "Oh—yes, you get a free ten-day trial," or something like that. But nope, I was wrong. You get it all—free.

Yesterday I signed up! Starting off easy—did about five different machines yesterday—only ten to twenty reps and with very light resistance that I could manage. My shoulders felt better last night.

Today my lower back was really bothering me. So after lunch I went back to the health club. Did the same machines with a few more reps. Then I got into the whirlpool for fifteen minutes. That was heaven!

I work from my house, so I still had to come back to work, but my back feels much better. I figure if I keep this up, I will be stronger in six weeks. Maybe getting some muscle back will reduce the pain. (I take Advil—but can't take the hard stuff pain pills.)

I hope this little story inspires someone else to find a way to get to a health club whatever your age. I think it is wonderful.

Betty N of El Cerrito, California, has survived serious health problems by focusing on the many positive features in her life.

> *Having had a liver transplant eighteen years ago, I renewed my feeling that "now is the only time there is" and you'd better enjoy whatever you are doing and the people you are doing things with. I just had a terrible fracture, requiring surgery and rehab, and it was wonderful how friends and family rallied around to help me and my husband. I am fortunate in having Kaiser Permanente medical insurance, which has provided complete coordinated care for over twenty-five years.*
>
> *We all face losses, of friends, family, and our own abilities, but rather than focus on these, I feel you can acknowledge them and continue to enjoy whatever activities that you relish.*

Maryanne S of Philadelphia, Pennsylvania, observed:

> *Some people become their illness. They allow it to consume the entirety of their being. They always say "yes, but" when suggestions are made as to how they may ease the burden of their illness, they prefer to carry it in a heavy sack on their back. Some people get a secondary gain from their illness—attention, sympathy, pity—that they may not get when they are well. Maybe they believe that less is expected of them when they are ill than when they are well, or when they are coping with their situation.*

There are many ways to be ill. Some people work hard at continuing with their lives, trying as hard as they can to push it to the back burner. Others go into complete denial, which can mean they don't adequately care for themselves. Some hide their illness from the world as though it is a mark of weakness. Then there are the "poor me" people who spend lots of energy feeling sorry for themselves. What is the right way to manage illness and infirmity? There is no right or wrong way. You have to find the way that is best for you. Here is one way:

Chiqui S of Lafayette Hills, Pennsylvania, was diagnosed with breast cancer twenty years ago, when cancer was often considered a terminal disease rather than a chronic one. To be a cancer survivor was often not a realistic aspiration. She was frightened, devastated, anxious. For Chiqui, a support group greatly helped her deal with her fears, outlook, and manner of dealing with breast cancer. Despite the fact that Chiqui is a nurse, when the disease became her own, she was as much at a loss as anyone might be.

When I got that diagnosis, I felt bereft and lonely. I had no one to talk to about it. Of course, I talked to my husband and children and that helped, but it didn't ease my fears. A friend told me about a twelve-week support group at Jefferson Hospital in Philadelphia that was being led by a social worker. I didn't know any of the women in the group. There were ten of us, ranging in age from thirties to sixties, all of different races and religions. Since we were getting chemo and losing our hair, she invited a wig maker to talk about our hair options. A psychologist spoke about mastectomies and lumpectomies and what that would mean in our lives. She also invited a clothing expert, a cosmetologist to help us with makeup—various other professional people who could help us deal with our concerns. One week our mates were invited, another week my daughters were invited. I don't actually remember the dialog, but we did a lot of talking about how we were feeling, how we would see the world, how the world would see us now that we had cancer.

After the twelve weeks were up, seven of us decided to continue to meet, weekly at first, then monthly. One woman moved to Chapel Hill, North Carolina, and then there were six. Over the years, we tried to contact her but never could find her. One of the women had sobbed the entire twelve weeks but must have found the group helpful because she continued with us. Our group has been meeting for twenty years.

We talked about things that you could only talk about with women who were going through this. We talked about our health issues, our changed bodies, our relationships with our mates, our fears; would we die soon, would we suffer? Did every pain mean the cancer had spread? Am I still physically attractive? Would a man want to fondle my breasts? We didn't talk often about sex, but it certainly was the elephant in the room. The woman who sobbed had a second mastectomy and reconstruction. Two of the women have died—and now there are four. We meet less frequently now, but we do still get together.

Twenty years is a long time for a support group to continue meeting. Why do you think that has happened?

These are things we can't talk to anyone else about. It is so important to have each other. Together over the years we've been through cancer recurrences, metastases, extramarital affairs, a husband who left when a second diagnosis was made. Bad stuff and good stuff. We've bonded, we care about each other, and this group has served a great need for us. It has been an important part of my life.

We don't always think of support groups as a prescription for healing an illness. But we know that the consequences of a serious disease affect far more than your body. This group has been a positive experience—a healing experience— for all of the women. Together, they've weathered a hard jolt in their lives with more strength than they might have had without it.

We spoke to **Carol M** of Atlanta, Georgia, about her recent bout with cancer. So many women we talked to have had or now have cancer in their lives—few were immune—whether through a spouse, a partner, or themselves. Is this a contagious disease?

When my daughter was advised to have a hysterectomy, she knew that I, who lived three thousand miles away, would be alarmed, anxious, and scared. And believe me, I was. My daughter is a born investigator, whether it's a refrigerator or her ovaries, and she got to work.

Is this surgery really necessary, who is the most qualified doctor, which is the best hospital, when is the right time to do it, what is the prognosis, what will this mean for my family? She searched the Internet for reliable sources, picked the brains of friends who might be able to offer good (and professional) advice, and got a second opinion. There were several doctors' visits, some options to consider, and many opportunities for confusion.

She started a notebook. As you might suspect, she had lots of questions and had them in hand when she went to the doctor. She took notes at all conversations with her doctors, then came home and rewrote the notes so that she would be able to understand later, and then put them into a file on her computer. What she didn't understand became the questions for her next visit.

Back to me, her worried mom. She e-mailed all her notes to me so I would know everything that was going on. This was extremely important to me. I knew that she was being completely truthful with me because that's the agreement that we have. When I got the good news that the prognosis was good, I trusted that this was the truth. I told her that if the news had not been good, I would have weathered it. After all, I've lived a long time, and maybe aging has an upside. All those years of experience have made me pretty strong.

Fast forward ten years. Two and a half years ago I was diagnosed with peritoneal cancer. Now I was alarmed, anxious, and scared for myself. I wasn't sure I would live through the winter. I had never been ill with anything really serious. So I used my daughter as my model. I never forgot how much I appreciated the notes she had sent me. I realized how much goes unheard and unnoticed when I was being bombarded with information I didn't want to hear and too emotionally overwhelmed to process it. I tried to always go to doctors' visits with someone close to me because I knew that two heads would be listening, asking questions, and taking notes. I combed the Internet for information. I asked so many questions that one of my favorite doctors reprinted a recent scholarly article about new thinking for me to help me decide on a direction to take going forward. I knew that the illness had life-changing consequences, and I needed the most and best information if I was going to plan well and get good care.

I got excellent care, and I'm a healthy cancer survivor—so far. The support of my family and friends still brings me to tears. I sleep well at night. My days are rich and full. I wish I never had cancer, but I did. (Do? Did?) That's always the question.

WHAT IS THE BEST RX FOR HEALTH?

There is machinery to diagnose our diseases, medicine to cure our bodies, insight to understand our minds, compassion to heal our souls, support to hold us up. All have their place. These all come from the outside. We hope our doctors look past our diseases to the rest of who we are. What comes from within, however, is probably the most important of all. Our inner resources are what get us through the rough patches, whether they be a summer shower or a tempest in our lives.

The key words here are

- knowledge

- truth

- participation

- trust

People probably face illness, physical limitations, and impairments—their own and those of the ones they care about—in the same ways they face other difficulties in their lives. People who are in the habit of searching out **knowledge** will do so in this situation, and the outcome will be more positive because they will, if nothing else, keep their doctors on their toes. People who insist on facing the **truth**, no matter how much it hurts, will benefit because they will make the most effective plans for dealing with these life-altering situations. Proactive people who **participate** in their diagnosis and treatment will gravitate to the most responsive doctors and form better relationships with them. Finally, knowledge, truth, and participation will engender **trust** in your doctors and family, giving you the confidence that you are getting the best medical care available.

9

SEPARATION AND LOSS ARE FACTS OF LIFE

How Do I Handle Them?

The past is our definition. We may strive, with good reason, to escape it, or to escape what is bad in it, but we will escape it only by adding something better to it.

— Wendell Berry

For all of us, this is surely the ultimate question—not *whether* we will suffer separation and loss, but how we deal with these greatest challenges that life brings. The realization starts much earlier for some than for others, but for all of us fortunate enough to reach these years, the accumulation of losses is as inevitable as the unfolding of life itself. The good news is that the view from these years is so different from what it was when we were only a decade or so younger. But more about that later . . .

Separation for families in today's world differs dramatically from that of our parents and grandparents. When they left home, and so often their country of origin, the wrench was particularly painful, usually more for those left behind than those looking forward to new lives and opportunity. Think of what it must have meant before telephones (in our own grandparents' memory) never to hear loved voices again. No phone, no plane, no e-mail, no Skype. Today, separation is hard to achieve, even when it may be the goal!

Mostly we think of separation and loss as related but differing in impact and kind. Separation implies a temporary condition, one that can be adjusted from time to time and may even lead to a reuniting of people or situations. Loss, on the other hand, is permanent. Its effects, its imprint will always be with us, although scars eventually fade and even, when we're ready to allow it, produce feelings of happiness and joy along with memories.

How do people we interviewed deal with loss? And what does *loss* mean? Most immediately presumed we were speaking of permanent loss from death. On reflection, however, it became evident that retirement, career change, changing one's home, giving up treasured things, and losing the close proximity of one's children also conjure a deep sense of loss.

CAN YOU LOSE YOUR IDENTITY?

How far have you come in discovering who you are? The person who feels defined by her career or occupation can have a very hard time dealing with the loss of that position. It can be crushing to realize that many listeners or adherents may have been responding to our office, title, or position more than to our dazzling insights and wisdom. Losing the satisfaction of wielding authority or of addressing an admiring audience can lead to genuine bewilderment. Several retired college professors said wryly but wistfully, "It's as though no one is listening! Don't they realize that I'm speaking? Will anyone ever again listen to me? Will anyone ever write down everything I say?"

Thelma says that when walking down the street with her boss, Wilson Goode, the then-mayor of Philadelphia, he told her how he had taken a walk with a predecessor once removed. His predecessor told him to notice how few people already didn't even recognize him, and he had left office only four years earlier. It was a good lesson, the mayor said, about how quickly one could feel unimportant if public recognition meant too much.

Pat B has recently retired and moved to Philadelphia, Pennsylvania, from San Diego, California. We asked her about the pain of separation and loss when she not only retired from a rewarding and highly valued career but also permanently moved from a city and life that she cherished.

> Separation and loss were facts of life from the time I was seven years old, when my father died. At age eight, I was sent off to one boarding school and then another, and I still remember the hurt and anger I felt as a little child. I endured yet another painful separation when my marriage ended in divorce.

Pat has a PhD in religious studies, and when her career eventually took her to San Diego, California, she suffered yet another separation from her family and friends who lived on the East Coast. However, she savored the eclectic community that she became a part of. Diversity of age, religion, race, nationality, the norm of academic life, was the hallmark of her existence for many years in San Diego. When the time came to retire from her faculty position, she decided to return to her roots in Philadelphia so that she could be closer to her children and grandchildren. Though Pat remembers the agony of these difficult times, she also remembers that she survived them in a positive way.

> *I have had to learn to live with separation and loss from the time I was too young to understand what was happening. But I learned to cope. The story of Jacob wrestling with the angel has great meaning for me because I see its wisdom and truth. Jacob had to leave the land of his uncle and go to the land of his father—and he received a new name, which was Israel. The interpretation of this that holds so much meaning for me is that*

every loss holds within it a wound and a blessing, and with each blessing comes a new name. When a fetus is born, it leaves the warmth and comfort of the womb—a wound—but it enters the world—a blessing—and it gets a new name: baby. Now you're toddling along and you're going to fall (the wound), but look at the blessing of independence and your new name: toddler. When the child enters school, he is torn away from his mother—a wound—but he learns wondrous things about the wider world—a blessing—and he gets a new name: student.

When I was first sent away to a Montessori boarding school in Bucks County, Pennsylvania, I knew something terrible was about to happen, and I ran away and hid in the bushes so my mother and aunt wouldn't find me. Of course, they did, and off I was sent in a car with a stranger. And I cried. However, in a while I learned to love my life at the school, and I also learned that between wound *and* blessing *is another state of being, and that is* chaos. *In all of the losses I have sustained, there was always this progression: wound, chaos, blessing.*

The knowledge and wisdom Pat has gained from her painful experiences of separation and loss have helped her cope with her current wound, blessing, and the chaos in between. Chaos is the state in which you learn to cope, find out what is good or bad or needs to be avoided or embraced. Although chaos is often the most painful part of loss, it is also the most necessary for healing the wound. There is no way to get from wound to blessing without the chaos in between.

Pat feels she is recovering from the wound of her retirement and move across the country by dealing with the chaos that has preceded the blessing and her new name: *retired Philadelphian.* The blessing is the closeness to her children and grandchildren and participating more in their lives. Pat continued:

So after two years I'm still dealing with the chaos between the wound and the blessing. Retired Philadelphian *is a new name I haven't quite learned to love yet. I miss university teaching.*

Opportunities to teach are not as readily available as I'd like. I miss the diversity of my preretirement world in San Diego. Now I'm mostly involved with people who are very much like me in age, gender, race, and nationality and wish I weren't. I write, I play games, I read. I look for places to teach. But I refuse to be busy for the sake of being busy just so I can avoid being by myself. I find that I'm often bored and restless. I need more structure to my life, and now I have to design my own structure. Maybe I'm lazy, maybe I have less energy, maybe I'm not used to creating structure since it was always at my fingertips without searching for it.

PEOPLE ARE ON THE MOVE

Geography can separate us in an eyeblink. How many families do you know whose grown children live in the same city? In the city where they were born? In the city where their parents live? Probably not many.

Barbara F had this to say:

When I was forty-two, I realized that I had devoted the first half of my life to making attachments and the rest of it would be spent making separations. A bleak, if oversimplified, observation, but mostly true nonetheless. My husband, three children, and I had moved across the country, tearing ourselves for the first time from family, friends, and the city of our birth. The wound was jagged and took a long time to heal. Especially for me. Our children were in seventh, eleventh, and twelfth grades, respectively, and it was a harsh break.

When your children bleed, you hemorrhage.

At first I thought, "How could I not have known how hard this would be?" At second, I thought, "I can't let this ruin the family. We've got to make it work."

There was no e-mail, Facebook, texting, tweeting, or Skype, and flying across country was still kind of a big deal. Even long-distance calling required some serious thought. So I felt really isolated out there in Berkeley, where I didn't know the ropes: how to be a parent during the wild counterculture seventies, living in the heart of hippie-land. Those were the minuses.

Here are the pluses. My husband kept telling me that our kids are good, solid kids with strong values. They'll find their way. We had been all over the world with our children; their comfort zones were very broad. We had raised them to believe that the whole world was their backyard.

There was also a move to Milwaukee, Wisconsin, wasn't there?

Yes, but that was after the children had finished high school. Although we moved from Berkeley, one daughter stayed, went to university there, and still lives in the bay area.

Fast forward to now. In the interim, our children gained strength, learned to view the world from a wide perspective, found friends among disparate people, settled in England, Boston, and California (and I in Philadelphia and Sarasota), so our family spans six thousand miles. Yet we are very much in touch. This includes the seven now-adult grandchildren who are very good friends. This past October, seven grandchildren plus one "honorary" grandchild surprised me on my eightieth birthday by gathering with the rest of the family (except for one) in Boston and Maine. The grandchildren arrived from London, Hamburg, Glasgow, New York, San Francisco, St. Louis, and Oregon. Talk about mobile lives!

How do these families that started out six thousand miles apart stay together?

It took work. Frequent visits were a priority. We motor-tripped with the grandchildren. My children weren't afraid to put their children on planes when they were quite small, so we could spend lots of time together and really get to know each other. We also added e-mail, Skype, and other technology as it came along, which surely makes keeping in touch much easier. Besides, we really like each other.

We also held yearly family reunions—at the Jersey shore when the grandchildren were little, and later in Northern California, Lake Tahoe, Great Barrington, Maine, South Africa, Italy. Don't think I spent these vacations cooking and cleaning for all these people! The eight adults took turns cooking, shopping, and cleanup on an assigned day and were free on the other days. We also took turns minding the children all day, leaving everyone else free from responsibility on the days they weren't in charge. We did these chores in pairs but didn't pair up with our spouses. This was important! We made sure to pair up with an in-law so that we got to plan, shop, work, and spend time more with one we saw less frequently. The pair in charge often planned a project: making kites, tie-dyeing T-shirts, scavenger hunts. The kids loved it!

Of course we're three generations of adults now, and we don't put schedules on the fridge anymore. But we all still get together yearly. Now some of the grandkids have partners, and they come, too. Our last vacation was in Taos, New Mexico. This time, the rule was that nobody over thirty was allowed to cook. The two older generations provided the credit cards, but the kids did all the meals. The vacation was a hoot!

So about these separations during the last half of my life. Six thousand miles of separation from my children is not as painful as it used to be or as I anticipated it would be. I have been very surprised at how close I can remain to them even though the distance in miles is great. I have learned that geography is not destiny when it comes to those you love. The death of my husband, on the other hand, was as painful as I knew it would be. This is a bleak separation that time makes more palatable, but the hole in the heart remains.

Is my life better or worse since I am now living squarely in a mobile family? I like that my children and grandchildren are people who are willing to look in the far corners of the world for their places and that they're comfortable in many settings. I'm glad they didn't feel constrained or obligated to stay close to home (as I did). As for me, I have continued to live a life of my own that greatly satisfies, and I treasure my independence. All things considered, I like the choices we, the family, have made.

IT'S NOT JUST PEOPLE: LOSS TAKES MANY FORMS

Even what may seem a superficial loss can trigger strong emotional response and sadness. Just losing a cherished family keepsake or piece of jewelry representing a past attachment can evoke a host of associations and memories that suddenly seem threatened to disappear along with the object. **Judith LeFevre**, the professional downsizing expert you met earlier, reminded us again that when we are trying to scale down our possessions, we are going to have to make choices, some of which may be very painful. We must understand that the silver turns black and the clothes don't come back in style, but the photos capture the spirit forever. The loss of treasured possessions is always a source of emotional stress. But we must also keep in mind that although the objects may disappear, the memories always remain in our hearts.

GRIEF

Is there ever an upside to the grief that accompanies bereavement? *No.* Grieving is what it is, and the pain can be beyond description. When grief extends into long periods (many months, and in some cases years), professional help is called for and can be found in various places: family doctors, psychiatrists, spiritual or religious counselors, and others.

A two-year period is not unusual, particularly when the loss is of a partner of very long standing. Many women of our generation never lived alone. The young woman who left home for her own apartment in the 1950s was as unusual as the young woman of today who returns to her parents' home after college! Most of us left to get married or stayed home as we started to work, so the loss of one's partner also carries the challenges of being alone for the first time.

Shirley L of Philadelphia, Pennsylvania, told us:

I married him when I was twenty-one and lived with him for fifty-three years, and he handled everything. But at the same time, he taught me a lot. He taught me to be secure in myself and gave me so much confidence; he thought I could do anything. That was a very big gift he gave me. When he got sick, he trained me to handle everything. My only regret is that he didn't live to enjoy this time of life with me.

When Gilbert died I was in limbo for two years. I had a lot to do—to sell a building, find a new place to live, close a business, go through years of papers and documents. And no one else could do any of this. I sometimes think God does this to you. He gives you things to do to prevent you from sucking your own wounds.

Elena S's husband died after a life punctuated by roller-coaster periods of illness and remission. Showing great resolve and using his courage as an example, she managed to meet this challenge with humor and a refusal to complain:

I think of death as a natural part of life. It comes at some point. I feel saddened by the loss of him, but I'm not saddened by the

*death because I know it's got to happen. I just think that life is
so much more important.*

*How you die is also important. Not in pain. We welcomed and
encouraged visitors; even the night when he finally went into a
coma, we went into his room. Not knowing if he could hear us,
we talked to him. We played the kind of music he liked. He was
surrounded by everyone who was important to him.*

*He was very funny and open and never complained. The first
few years I didn't venture out much. I had many good woman
friends, and I think it was only because of them I was able to
reach some kind of equilibrium. I did a lot of crying—mostly to
myself. When I felt that I couldn't control my crying, I went to
the doctor and got myself a little antidepressant. It helped a lot.
Really. I think you need to know when you might need happy
pills. Actually, I was on it for a few years, and only in the past
six months have I finally taken myself off. I seem to be doing
fine, but it's taken that long. You may not show it outwardly or
even to yourself, but it's there. I think it's good to recognize
and admit it. To be open about it and not feel ashamed to feel
depressed.*

We met someone who could live in a world that combines yesterday and today constructively without depression and regret. Meet
Lore:

Lore Jonas was the widow of the acclaimed philosopher Hans
Jonas, whom she met when she was quite young, and he older, in
their hometown of Regensburg, Germany. In her nineties, Lore
appreciated the opportunity to talk about her life with Hans. The
war had driven them out of Germany—to Palestine, before the
state of Israel existed, then to Israel, Canada, and finally the United States as readers and admirers found places to welcome Hans
as a scholar and professor.

We found her, more than twenty years widowed, actively engaged in correspondence and business affairs with Hans's Euro-

pean and American publishers in addition to her own wide, serious reading of history and philosophy. She was living in a very large and beautiful retirement community that her children had found for her. She liked her comfortable apartment but found living there disappointing.

> *I believed that with so many people I would find interesting activities, but when people here have talks about books, they are current best-sellers, not the kind of serious reading I am used to and would like to discuss. Recently a wonderful poet was invited to speak—only fifteen people showed up! But I do have visitors fairly often, and I love seeing my children and grandchildren.*

Gesturing toward a pile of mail and books:

> *I keep quite busy with correspondence also. These are letters and reports from publishers who still print Hans's books all over the world, and from so many people he influenced and inspired. So although he has been gone since 1993, at age eighty-nine, I feel we are together in his work, which we always discussed. I read and reread all the love letters he ever wrote to me.*

You met **Hanne Minz** in chapter 2. Her professional growth and accomplishments can be seen in relief against the backdrop of losses endured along the way.

Hanne's life has been visited by profound losses from early on: first her mother, when Hanne was a seven-year-old in a small town in Sweden, and then her maternal grandmother in the same year. Her father sent Hanne and her brother, who was two years older, to boarding school in England that year—a new country, new people, and a new language all at once.

> *Loss shaped my early life. We learn how to be mothers from our mothers. There are so many things you lose when you lose your parents. Hopefully we can moderate our own behavior*

and learn to be good parents ourselves. My father remarried,
and his wife was not a good mother. Later I realized that that
may have been because she had lost her own mother when she
was a young adolescent.

Many years later, in her mid-sixties, Hanne went to England for a
boarding school reunion. It was a trip she and her husband had
planned to make together. Unfortunately, her husband had died
shortly before they were to travel.

At the reunion we realized we were all damaged by loss—some
were the children of diplomats who traveled or men who had
died in the war. We were at the school in 1951. We realized
that what we had in common was this shattering loss and that
we knew we had to rely on each other. While some have suc-
cumbed along the way, we've also accomplished a lot. Going to
boarding school was difficult—you had no one to comfort you
if you fell down—"Come on, get up. Stiff upper lip. Keep go-
ing!" Lots of dents and bruises along the way. No one to read
you stories and tuck you in and kiss you good night. I look
back and think I don't know how I did it, but it certainly made
me resilient.

Resilience and more was needed when Hanne and her own family were forced to deal with a recent crushing loss. More than ten
years ago, Hanne, her husband, her son Adam, and daughter
Marina were faced with thirty-year-old Adam's diagnosis of peritoneal mesothelioma. Adam was a fun-loving, 190-pound skier,
hiker, and professional chef. When Adam died two and a half
years later, he had wasted away to 125 pounds after a steady,
painful decline. Today Hanne is in her second term as chair of the
executive board of directors of the Mesothelioma Applied Research Foundation.

When Adam was first diagnosed I spent days and nights on the
Internet, calling researchers, and begging for Adam to be in-
cluded in any treatment available. There still is no effective

cure. Somehow, ingested asbestos fibers may have gone into his digestive tract. Just as some smokers or people exposed to tobacco smoke may never get cancer, (apparently) some people exposed to asbestos do not get mesothelioma. Now we know that every school he attended was contaminated. After damage in the 1994 earthquake in the San Fernando Valley, our home of thirty-two years had to be demolished and rebuilt. It was found to have transite, a common building material made from cement and asbestos. When the children were in middle school, they attended a new school where I designed and ran a program integrating the arts with the academic curriculum. Pottery was part of it, and Adam and Marina often stayed late to help me clean the pottery kilns with asbestos gloves. Even their high school was later rebuilt because asbestos was found there.

I do what I can to advance the mission of the Mesothelioma Applied Research Foundation to find a cure. I started with fund-raising. The first time I attended a symposium I took a whole stack of pictures of Adam. I asked researchers I met there to take one and put it in his or her lab to remind assistants that this is why they are working. I didn't want them to think of the people they are doing it for as anonymous. And now when I address the people at our symposia, I tell them that I know the worst thing is to be in the depth of our grief and know the injustice of our loss, but I remind them that we have patients there as part of the group as well, who are living with mesothelioma successfully—and that while the researchers are looking through their microscopes there are patients looking right back at them.

Is it Hanne's resilience, learned early on and strengthened through the years, that has enabled her to channel her grief in such a way that she has become a force for helping others who suffer as her son did? We see around us so many examples of people who survive tragedy best by using it to plant seeds of hope for others and find peace through doing it. They look at the world around them with new eyes, open to the lives and suffering of others and doing whatever they can to help.

Blanche Burton-Lyles' only child, a son, died suddenly when he was only thirty. Although she says that her strong faith never wavered, her profound grief, she felt, would never abate. Gradually, she realized that she was not only able to love and appreciate the wonderful drawings and humorous writings he had left, but that thinking about his whole life was a joy. Blanche says, "I was honored to be his mother." When she speaks of him, it is usually with a chuckle at the remembrance of his presence in the house.

There is an upside to emerging from grief, and that is as normal and to be expected as the grieving itself. **Carolyn Walter** began to write *The Loss of a Life Partner: Narratives of the Bereaved*[1] as a way to find meaning and to deal with the death of her husband twenty years ago, when he was forty-seven. As a professor at Widener University, Dr. Walter was asked to create a course for social work and psychology students on the subject of bereavement and loss; this important book preceded another for professionals in the field and addresses both the lay public as well as professionals.

The individual stories, in their own words, chronicle the experiences of partners in both traditional marriages and in nontraditional relationships such as gay/lesbian and cohabiting (unmarried) couples, which had considerably less societal support than they might today. Dealing with her own bereavement and watching as their children had to face the loss of their father, Carolyn became increasingly aware of both the universality of the experience and its deeply individual and personal aspects. And professionally, as both a counselor and professor, she sees the value of therapy for many people coping with loss. Carolyn told us:

I do see life as a journey. The loss of a partner isn't the end of life or the end of joy. I remarried very happily while I was writing the book. But it isn't the end of memory either, or of the trauma brought on by the loss. I think that it does make us aware of the importance of now, of using our time well, of realizing this moment will not last. The loss changes you: you're not the same person you were, but you can continue to grow—often in unexpected and positive ways.

Carolyn herself said that she learned a great deal from the people she interviewed for the book. She was very struck by the observations of a social worker in her late eighties:

The idea of no longer being the same person was evident to me in her experience. She realized that she wasn't the outgoing person she thought she was—that it had been her husband who was the one who talked to people when they traveled, and that she had gone along with him. Being alone enabled her to know more about herself—that she was much more comfortable than she had expected to be. She no longer thought of being alone as almost a sin.

Maryanne S's husband of Philadelphia, Pennsylvania, died when he was fifty-five years old.

My children were twenty-one and twenty-three when my husband died. There are two ways you can lose a spouse. One is suddenly and one is slowly. In my case it was over a period of five years. During that period we talked frequently about death. His was not the only major loss I experienced during my adult life. Loss in general for me has to do with the flip side of it. So when you lose it, it's a big hole. But I think the key for understanding loss is the other side. When you are experiencing the one you love, or the job you love, or the house you love, if you experience that love profoundly while you've got it, then losing it can be a sweet sad or a bittersweet sad. If you really appreciated it while you had it and you knew the time was limited, it exquisitely intensified the joy that you felt. And now, when you don't have it anymore, you look back on that excitement and pleasure and fun as a rare treasure and blessing.

If you haven't faced death together, or if you hadn't resolved some of the issues we all inevitably need to cope with in a relationship, problems arise when you suffer a loss. You have regrets because of what you could have or should have done to maximize your time together. And then you wind up compromising your current life. You can't make room for what's next because you're hung up on what you used to have and wish you had said or done. So basically I think there's a flip side to grief and loss, and that is the joy and the gifts.

My husband was not afraid to die. He had a wonderful five years after he was diagnosed, and we did as many things as we could. Once you really love someone and have a good experience, then that love stays, the experience stays. That helps you learn how to go on after that. I think of life as a yin and yang. With the negative energy comes positive energy.

It seems as though you were both mentally and emotionally prepared for Bob's death in that you faced it together –head-on. Most people think of mortality and the ephemeral nature of life in the abstract. We know we are mortal in our head, and that life is short. (It rolls off the tongue easily and often.) But do we really know it in our gut? You actually *experienced* his mortality for five years. Do you feel you learned about the yin and yang of death because you both lived through this?

I guess I have always been aware of the transience of everything in life. I think the expectation that what you have will last is faulty. Whatever is, is ephemeral. This is how he felt: "I had a loving marriage, I had a great job, I had great kids, I traveled, I did lots of community service, I had great parents." When he got sick, he fought very valiantly. But at the end, he was graceful, gracious, and not angry. He was grateful for what he had had because he knew he was more fortunate than most. We both wish he had had more time, but I think he wasn't afraid to give it up himself because he had never been afraid to live. He had lived fully with a great deal of passion and love for his friends, family, and colleagues, and that helped him as death approached. He didn't rage or fight at the end. He was incredibly gracious despite the indignities: the diapers and loss of control. He was only fifty-five! Friends were crying in my living room after they said good-bye to him. He educated so many people on how to die.

On looking back, I realize that I didn't learn all this when he died. I learned it all the time throughout our marriage and understood even more later on reflection. Our separate identities are what we created all along. My identity was not my husband or his job. I have my own identity. It didn't diminish our love for each other. He clarified that for me

I start by assuming that I am not entitled. Because I try to be a good person, behave moderately, and obey the law does not entitle me to any rewards beyond intrinsic ones. I believe everything is a gift that must be appreciated while it is mine— and it may not be mine forever because I am not entitled. How you deal with the death of your spouse is predicated on how you lived your life all along. I never said, "Poor me!" or "Why me?" It's totally random. What I say is, "Why not me?" There's no answer to that, and dwelling on that uses energy that's better used for coping. Loss is something we must accept, withstand, manage, and then keep growing. Loss helped me become much more compassionate to other people, to begin to understand some of the hardships they may be facing.

When I opened up to other people about my own losses, the potential for a friendship or a relationship was much more affecting, much more real, because loss is really the human condition. When we lose it, we were lucky to begin with and should be grateful for what we were given—and then make room for what's next. I mustn't think of what I have as permanent. I can't expect to have it forever. Sometimes I think that if loss doesn't come on a given day, that's a great day! I try to balance myself to expect that loss may come my way rather than being angry at how could this have happened to me. I look around and see that I have so much more than most people. My husband didn't have life after fifty-five, my daughter never had her birth parents, my son didn't have the opportunity to be healthy all his life. And yet I refuse to be defeated because I was given so much in life that's good.

Some people seem unable to get beyond their grief. Was their love greater than others'? Are they less resilient? Maybe fearful of facing the world without the person they lost? Too fragile to cope?

Well, some people become their loss. I think it's disingenuous to become your loss. I think you have to own your growth. What did I learn from my loss? I've been growing up, I've been growing old, I've been growing hair on my chin. If you don't grow, then you're not alive anymore. So you have to constantly look at the model that as we grow, we change. We find ways to nourish ourselves, and that helps to counterbalance the loss. Try to learn something new each day; plan to do something each day that feeds your soul.

To be reflective every day about what's new, what's surprising, what's sad; to do an inventory of the events in your life. To try to do something self-affirming every day—read, travel, help someone else, knowing that whatever you have today might not be there tomorrow. Keep open to a wide range of possibilities. Those you love might not be there tomorrow. That's why it helps to love a lot of people. I like to check back on people who have meant a lot to me in other parts of my life and to make room for new people.

My network with people, the connections I keep helped me tremendously with the many losses in my life. I started a women's group about twenty-eight years ago that still meets monthly. I think I did this because I don't have sisters. We're all going through different experiences, and we draw on each oth-er for help. Some of us have moved, changed jobs, gotten di-vorced, been widowed, dealt with childbirth, parents' deaths, children's illnesses, been thin then fat, retired, all kinds of things. Our group is like a think-tank sisterhood of friendship. We don't all agree on everything, ever, but we care about each other. We laugh at each other, and we're able to be honest with each other. It has been such an incredible foundation. We nev-er expected it to last this long.

Is Maryanne a Pollyanna? Not at all. She's the opposite of a Pol-lyanna. Her take on life is that she is no more entitled to the gifts she has been given than the next person. Good breaks and bad breaks befall us in random order; how we cope determines the quality of our lives. It's up to us to grow, reach, and survive our injuries.

The oldest women we interviewed are **Julie K** of Philadelphia, Pennsylvania, one hundred, and **Thelma G** of Redwood City, California, ninety-eight. Julie says, "Hardly anyone who knows me will be left to attend my funeral!" Both, of course, have sustained many losses and dealt with many serious challenges. Yet both very similarly have reached a vantage point, a perspective that enables each to speak of the losses and their sense of the ending, calmly and smiling, without any apparent bitterness or fear, "It's all part of life."

SOME GOOD NEWS

At the beginning of this chapter, we said the view of all of this is different from here than it would have been a decade or so earli-er. Just the fact that we are thinking about how we live, how far we've come, and what we've learned and are still to learn is mak-ing the difference. We still discover meaning and purpose in this gift of time. Indeed, we recognize it as a gift not to be squandered. We've developed resources for coping with profound change and realize that we really are stronger than we were.

Sister Marina B, OSBM, in her seventies, is the director of the Basilian Spirituality Center in Fox Chase Manor, Pennsylvania. Her sense of humor is manifested in the poster behind her desk, which says,

"Please, Lord, keep your arm around my shoulder and your hand over my mouth."

(Sister Marina says everyone who sees it wants one.) She is planning an icon-painting workshop entitled "Blessings from Chaos" and realizes, she says, that "we learn as much from darkness as from light and how wonderfully we are made." For her, Psalm 139 expresses this:

> Your hand will guide me,
> Your right hand hold me fast.
> If I say, "Surely darkness shall hide me,
> and night shall be my light,"
> Darkness is not dark for you
> and night shines like the day.
> Darkness and light are but one.

10

SOMETIMES I FEEL SAFEST IN MY SENIOR BUBBLE

My World Is Shrinking. How Do I Expand It?

A man grows most tired while standing still.

—Chinese proverb

What does intergenerational mean in your life?

Are you happily living among other people who are mostly your age? Do you interact on a deeper than superficial level with others who are much younger or older? We've been talking to some retirees who say the thing they miss most about their work lives is the interaction they had with colleagues or coworkers of various ages. Are younger people interested enough to listen to you? Do you enjoy listening to them? How do we cross the generational divide? Should we? What do you think?

Once retired, some people tend to pursue interests and activities primarily with their contemporaries. This phenomenon is a result of *temptation* and *opportunity*.

IT'S SO TEMPTING TO TAKE THE EASY WAY

The temptation is to follow the path of least resistance. It is always easiest to remain in one's comfort zone and surround ourselves with people our own age. This was expressed in one of our workshops in a recorded discussion:

> We know how our contemporaries think, talk, and behave. We can predict their reactions to the things we do and say. Our friends rarely challenge us to rethink our long-held beliefs, our values, our ethos. If they do, it's easier to ignore what those friends say and keep agreeing with the many other people we know who tend to validate our ways of thinking. I'm embarrassed to say this, but I think I'm drawn to people who agree with me more than to people who don't.

> I don't quite understand the reasons why people who are younger than I am take a different path than their parents took. Sometimes I think it's just a way for the next generation to show their independence. I'm not convinced of the merits of the changes that are happening all around me. I think our kids are making some big mistakes. They could so easily learn from us. What worked for us could work for them.

Many other women told us that they feel demeaned by the patronizing way younger people sometimes deal with them. They think that younger people view them as old-fashioned, passé, and maybe even "losing it."

> I don't hear so well, and sometimes kids talk fast and I need to ask them to repeat what they've said. They're very impatient and think I don't "get it." Well, I don't—not because I haven't understood, but because I haven't heard what they said. I find myself nodding and agreeing rather than constantly asking them to repeat. So, in a way, I just retreat.

Some get the feeling that younger people believe it's time for us to move out of the way so they can make their marks in the world. We had our chance; now it's their turn. The temptation is to seek solace in each other, and so we tend to seek out our contemporaries by choice.

Robin J, a blogger from the state of Alabama, has thought about both the content and manner of communicating across generations:

> *I don't think interest in listening is relegated only to younger people. I think many age groups do not want to listen to anyone other than those who agree with them and their choices. Do I enjoy listening to them? Sometimes yes, and sometimes, no. As I age, I believe in generational division because that is the one thing on which we agree. My beliefs and those of my peers are more relevant to me than to others of differing age groups. I am more experienced simply because I have engaged and overcome many situations others have not. I have experienced death of loved ones, friends, careers ending, empty nests, physical frailty—temporary and long term—and am still capable of facing life each day.*

But do you find that people want to hear about other people's problems?

> *Actually, yes. There are many people who want to hear of those experiences, if only for encouragement and courage to face their own struggles. But for those who have not experienced, what seems to many, hurtful issues, they are not as likely to want to listen to me. I accept that they are just not "there" yet and for some, they never will be. Should we try to cross the divide? Yes, but only if those we are speaking to want to hear us. There is a possibility that our trying to force others to hear our voice might result in resentment in the hearer and frustration in the sharer.*

ARE THERE OPPORTUNITIES TO HANG OUT?

Once we retire, where do we find the younger folks who peopled our lives? Conversations by the water cooler are no longer part of our days:

- Conversations that helped us understand what's current in the world

- Discussions about new young authors who chronicle our times from a fresh perspective and with a new writing style

- Conversations that criticize or embrace but that at least talk about social networking and navigating life online

- Professional meetings in which issues and events that impinged on our work now no longer inform our thinking

Without the face-to-face daily encounters, how do we engage in a casual exchange of ideas, know what styles are in or weird, figure out the subtleties which mark us as belonging—or not—to the world?

Chic and trendy may not be our goal.

But neither do we want to personify the appearance, language, and behaviors that reinforce age stereotypes. When we isolate ourselves from a whole segment of society, even our lexicon remains in a time warp. Because we don't often have conversations with young people about what is meaningful to *their* lives, we may not learn current ways to express ourselves. Language is fluid and shifts with the times. We may become bereft of fresh ideas that give old words new meaning. In fact, many women at our workshops felt that the young actually speak a different language. Conversational bridges between generations seem, for many, to have become bridges too far. When communication is strained, the distance between generations widens. Somehow television and magazines don't fill that gap, especially now that even they are fading as sources of news.

Also heard at one of our workshops was this lament, repeated frequently by many others:

> *The Internet and new technological gadgets dominate the conversations I have with younger people. Well, maybe it doesn't dominate the conversation, but it seems that they look at the world through the prism of technology—how they get news, how they exchange ideas, how they organize their lives, how they get information, how they relate to each other—and I don't know that vocabulary, so I have trouble communicating with them. So it seems I just don't have much to talk about with younger people.*

Maybe this seems unimportant. Maybe remaining current in and of itself is not a value to be sought. However, as seniors close out the wider community, they increasingly tend to become more isolated within the perimeter of their society, a society that becomes smaller and more limited as time passes. Obviously, the inevitable infirmity and death of their contemporaries will continue to reduce their world even as they are further shut out of a huge segment of society—those younger than they. By decreasing their contact and involvement with the world, seniors often become increasingly self-involved and inwardly focused. And suddenly they notice that their world has shrunk. How do they expand it? Can they reverse it? Can it be avoided before it happens?

Another workshop attendee added this:

> *I don't like that most of the people I know are in my age group. I like to be stimulated by being with people of all ages. I used to teach in a high school, and although the kids were often off the wall, I miss their spirit and energy, their humor and optimism. But they don't want to spend time with me. Even the thirty- and forty-year-olds on my street look on me as some kind of*

relic. And I'm only sixty-five! They don't consider me a social friend or invite me in for a glass of wine as they do each other. They are respectful to us in a patronizing way. But that's not what I want, and I'm not sure how to go about keeping them in my life.

This chapter contains the stories of women who refused to let it happen. Meet **Gale C** of Boston, Massachusetts.

Gale's condo overlooks the Boston skyline. She had recently moved there from another apartment because this one had a better view and she loves the vista. Her friends thought this was a crazy undertaking for a seventy-eight-year-old widow. They could understand a move, say, to a retirement community, but not this. It smacked of youth and energy and future, and they thought it was time for her to put that behind her. What if she gets ill? What if she can't drive? What if it snows? Gale tut-tutted at all this. "What if I don't? What if I can? So what if it snows!"

Gale retired fourteen years ago from her career as a medical librarian. She is surrounded by photos of her children and grandchildren, carefully collected art objects, and unusual items from her travels around the world. The last thing she wants to do is retire from the world. In fact, Gale works hard at expanding her world the deeper she gets into retirement.

We had traveled to Cambodia, where we were wowed by the country, culture, and the people. We were greatly moved by the horrors the people were still suffering following the devastation of the Vietnam War. After we returned, we connected with an American who was privately financing a hospital in Cambodia. We asked what we could do to help. Money, money, money! Books, books, books! It was a hospital with no library. Fortunately, we could donate a bit of money. But even more fortunately for me, I saw an opportunity to donate my skills as a medical librarian. That decision was a life changer for me.

I started to amass medical books and journals and shipped them to Cambodia. Locating the books and journals created opportunities, interactions with people, and experiences that were very enriching in themselves. After sending seventy boxes, I told my husband that I had to go over there and see what was happening to them. My husband was unwilling to go with me because the harsh conditions in Cambodia made a trip there too difficult for him. This was in the early nineties, and Cambodia still had not recovered from the war. "Well," I said. "I gotta go!" And I went—alone.

I see you are surrounded by all these cartons and piles of books and journals. They must be on their way to Cambodia. But I also see that you have such interesting objects, sculptures, art of all sorts.

People have been so helpful. I'm amazed that all you have to do is ask, and people with things to give come forward. Many of these art objects are gifts.

Your work must be very appreciated there. How did you accomplish this?

I worked there ten days and ten nights, trained a librarian, and together we developed the first English-language library in the country. It is now considered the best, and the medical school sends its students to this library.

Here's an aside: the medical school library has French journals and books. The students want English medical books. The medical school in Cambodia is financed by the French, and they threaten to withhold money if the medical books in the library are not in French. So the students use the hospital library instead of the medical school library because the books and journals are in English.

Then my husband died, and my life changed. I now know that I owe an apology to all my widowed friends. I was not caring enough about them when they became widowed. I did not realize the devastation of widowhood. But my work in Cambodia was a lifesaver.

This project has given me a focus in my retirement. Look, you can't help the whole world. But if you pick one little thing, or one little place, you can make a difference. And that's what I've done. I feel people are missing so much when they don't go beyond themselves and give.

Gale looks on this time in her life as an opportunity. Her energy seems boundless.

I had four children in four years, and while they were growing up I had no time for me. I regret, for their sakes and mine, that they were so close in age. It wasn't fair to them, and it wasn't fair to me. When they were in high school and college, I went back for a master's degree. I felt that I deserved some time to travel and be selfish. But I also found that I need to be always looking beyond my life and seeing what else there is to do out there in the world.

Paola Gianturco of Mill Valley, California, has had many careers in her very productive lifetime. And she's not finished yet.

My first thirty-four working years had been spent in public relations, advertising, marketing, corporate communications, development, and strategies—always on the business side. I also taught an eight-day course at Stanford about women and leadership and then taught that course within corporations, for which the students got credit at Stanford. I was fifty-five at the time and exhausted. I had lots of frequent flyer miles, and I took what I thought was going to be a one-year sabbatical.

I never went back to the corporate world.

On my sabbatical I did what I loved to do most, which was photography and travel. And so I set out on my next career and became a photojournalist. I decided to explore the world, photographing and interviewing women on several continents who were starting their own microbusinesses. It was a big change for me. I had to learn how to write because up to then, I had only written business reports. I'm now seventy-three, and since that sabbatical I've published five books.

A career U-turn! From development work in big corporations to photojournalism, focusing on microbusinesses. And these are very small businesses, started by poor women in poor countries.

Paola, how did you got involved in the grandmother movement that led to your most current book, *Grandmother Power: A Global Phenomenon*[1] ?

The movement was under way, but no one was documenting it. I didn't generate the grandmother movement. However, I took it a step further by enabling those empowered women to go beyond their own communities and themselves, linking them with women in first-world countries who became their partners. Now women all over the world could be connected and share their ideas.

I was interested in it not just because I'm a grandmother, but because I am always looking for stories about how women are changing the world and creating hope and possibilities in very difficult circumstances. These are stories that are not often told. I found that in Kenya, grandmothers are raising grandchildren, sometimes ten or twelve at a time, who have been orphaned by AIDS. The future of the continent of Africa may rest in the hands of these grandmothers. It made me wonder what grandmothers are doing in other countries.

Nobody seems to be talking about what grandmothers are doing. I've traveled to fifteen countries in Africa, the Middle East, North and South America, and Europe and found that around the world, women were saying, "This is not good enough for my grandchildren." They were finding pressing local issues that disturbed them—and doing something about it. In Africa, it was the practice of female genital mutilation. In India, they were becoming solar engineers. In Argentina, they were reading in schools. There are now eight thousand grandmothers in Canada raising money for the African grandmothers group. In Grandmother Power, I have documented the grandmother movement around the world.

All of my books have been about women. I've now documented their lives in fifty-five countries. One hundred percent of my royalties go to philanthropic programs, to whatever projects the women I interview are working on. Book number four was about women running nonprofit organizations in fifteen countries. The money from that book went to the Global Fund for Women. Book number two was about celebrations and festivals all over the world. It was fascinating to me because despite their roles and behavior in these festivals, women are so often discounted. All of my royalties from that went to the International Museum of Women. The thread running through all of my books is their description of women's lives around the world and the philanthropic work they do.

I am particularly interested in *Grandmother Power: A Global Phenomenon* because of its focus on a time in women's lives when they are past sixty, when much of the world thinks they're finished contributing, that they no longer have anything important to do. You are so enthusiastic about their empowerment, by the value of what they do. Paola, I find it interesting and exciting that it was my granddaughter, Carla Fleisher, who knew of your work and your book, and told me that you and I must connect. Maybe there is more intergenerational interest than I had thought.

I hope so. We grandmothers do have a lot more to give. I certainly found that as I covered the globe. I found that it's not in spite of but because of their age that the 120 women I've interviewed bring wisdom and perspective to their lives and to the lives of others that was not possible for them to contribute as younger women.

When Paola spreads her stories about these women around the world, she empowers us all. Here is another of many stories by women who have welcomed this stage of life with the imagination to see possibilities, the energy to seize opportunities, and the will to include the wider world in their vision.

Chiqui S reported her experience in Tibet.

I am a retired nurse who over my career worked in a general hospital setting as a corporate nurse for the DuPont Company and for the last ten years as the director and coordinator of volunteers for two different hospices.

When I was seventy-four, I joined an international medical organization that coordinates volunteer medical missions to needy communities worldwide. My husband, a physician, was unable to go with me, so I went alone.

Our destination was the Drepung Loseling Monastery and sur-rounding Tibetan refugee settlements in Mundgod, in the south of India. I flew to Mumbai, then transferred to a big city, Hubli-Dharwad, where a van was waiting to take us—two medical doctors, a pharmacist, another registered nurse, and me—to the Tibetan settlement in Mundgod, which was two hours further from Hubli. We provided health care to hun-dreds of sick and needy monks, nuns, and Tibetan laypeople. The clinic provides free examinations, consultations, and dis-count medications to people who have fled from Tibet to escape Chinese oppression.

Our medical team, four doctors and four nurses, worked from dawn to dusk, in ninety-five-degree weather, with just ceiling fans for comfort. We brought bandages, Band-Aids, nebulizers, antibiotics, nonprescription pain medications, lotions, salves, and over five hundred pairs of used eyeglasses. Those patients

*who were diagnosed with more serious conditions, such as ap-
pendicitis, kidney stones, bone fractures, and acute angina
could not be treated at the clinic and had to be transported by
van to a large general teaching hospital two hours distant from
the clinic.*

*In 1949, when China invaded Tibet, India's prime minister
Nehru allowed the Dalai Lama, his court of advisors, and
thousands of Tibetan citizens to set up a temporary government in India. Now, sixty-two years later, Tibetans are still
living in India with very little hope of returning to Tibet,
which remains under Chinese rule.*

*Some of the ethical teachings of the Dalai Lama were incorpo-
rated into our program and ultimately into my life:*

- *Nonviolence is essential for solving man-made conflicts of
  war, destruction, and repression.*
- *Gentleness should be chosen over violence, no matter how
  bad the oppression is.*
- *Kindness is a must for keeping the world livable.*
- *Courage is required to struggle.*
- *Compassion is required to mitigate the struggles of other
  people.*

*I worked very hard during my time at the clinic, but the two
weeks in India gave me a broad approach toward living. To be
able to care for 180 people per day in ninety-five-degree heat
with only ceiling fans moving the hot air around for relief, I
learned to meditate and did it every morning. I felt that I was
actually too old for this kind of work under these kinds of
circumstances. But I saw it through and can look back and say
that this experience was a life changer, and I will always be
thankful for that transformative time in my life.*

Chiqui's story teaches us that transformative experiences can
come at any age. In this experience, she learned not only her

limitations but also her possibilities. There is never a stage in our lives in which we are too taut to stretch and bend—if not physically, then spiritually. We grow as we stretch our minds and hearts. Chiqui grew by making a difficult commitment and continuing to give, even when it became apparent to her that she had overestimated her physical strength. It's three years later, and Chiqui is still giving.

At eighty, **Blanche Burton-Lyles's** life is linked firmly to her past, but most important today is how she is able to connect it creatively and productively to the present and future. (Dear Reader: Please use your imagination. This is where we should have an accompanying CD of Blanche playing Rachmaninoff and another of the glorious contralto voice of Marian Anderson singing at the Metropolitan Opera. They have been intertwined for nearly all of Blanche's life.)

Blanche's mother was her first piano teacher. Mrs. Burton realized that although she was an accomplished musician who often accompanied the great contralto at their Union Baptist Church, Blanche's prodigious talent required more advanced teaching while she was still a child in elementary school.

How did your career in music start?

> Whenever Miss Anderson was in Philadelphia, she would invite me to come to her house and play for her guests after her concerts. When I was still in elementary school, she spoke to people at Curtis Institute of Music who had me play for them and offered me a scholarship. I was the first young girl, the first African American, and the youngest (by a few months) student so privileged. The only younger person was Gary Graffman. I was accommodated by attending junior high and high-school classes outside in the mornings and studying at Curtis every afternoon. It was wonderful.

While she had significant experiences as a young concert pianist appearing with symphony orchestras and in solo appearances, Blanche followed her parents' advice and earned a degree that would enable her to teach in public schools as well.

> *I did know there were barriers because of race. I remember when Mother and I were invited to stay with a very wealthy family in Connecticut. My teacher, Mme. Vereskova, had agreed to have me play for a worthy cause there and accompanied us. It was obvious that the family had no idea that we were African American. When we arrived, they awkwardly said they were awfully sorry but it turned out they didn't have room for us in their enormous house. Fortunately, they found a family who were gracious enough to have us on very short notice. I did go on to be the first African American woman to play with the New York Philharmonic at Carnegie Hall.*
>
> *But I never regretted taking my parents' advice and making sure I had the security of a bachelor's degree and the ability to teach. I loved working with the teachers and the children of all ages until I retired in my sixties. But I was able to continue to play for audiences and to pursue my interest in helping serious young vocal artists.*

When is "retirement" not "retirement?" This may sound like a riddle, but the answer in Blanche's case is simple: when it's a period of work and commitment that grows seamlessly out of a life's calling. Fast forward to today and roughly a mile or so from the house where Blanche grew up, which she rebuilt to accommodate her aging parents' needs and her own life after divorce; you are likely to find her, petite and elegantly dressed, in a nineteenth-century two-story house on South Martin Street in south Philadelphia. The street is now named Marian Anderson Way, and the house has a plaque announcing that it is the Marian Anderson Historical Residence & Museum (on the National Register of Historic Places, US Department of the Interior).

Blanche's beat goes on.

Blanche has always felt a deep connection to Marian Anderson and gratitude for her interest and mentorship. She remembers fondly playing as a child for Anderson's guests at parties given in the house after the singer's concerts at the nearby Academy of Music. Miss Anderson owned several houses on the block and was born in one around the corner. Blanche not only bought and restored the residence but created the Marian Anderson Historical Society, Inc., and the nonprofit organization that followed. As its founder and president, with the help of corporate and individual sponsors she has inspired to help, she has been able to mentor and promote the careers of young vocal artists in memory of her own mentor.

Visitors to the house will usually hear recorded music as they examine the treasures and memorabilia, but if asked, Blanche will probably sit down at her grand piano and play. She has also been appearing on college campuses, taking with her one of the young vocal artists in the scholars' program she founded.

Blanche understands better than most Rachmaninoff's words: "Great music is enough for a lifetime, but a lifetime is not enough for great music."

Seeing and working with talented young people gives Blanche much more than a way of "giving back," although that was surely in her mind when she started. Her enthusiasm and appreciation for young people in the arts is coupled with the experience and sophistication it takes to see what they need. Knowing how to help them ("We may even have to help some know how to dress.") and doing it is making for a wonderful life and a clear and positive view of the future. She laughs when she says she expects to live to 105. But she means it because she has so much to do.

TRAVEL WITH A PURPOSE

Jean A misses the structure provided by her preretirement schedule and even more misses being with "bright young people." She has found that the kind of traveling she loves provides an opportunity to interact with younger people because she is usually the oldest volunteer in the group.

> *I like to travel with a purpose; it may be a trivial purpose or for my own enrichment, but if I can do something that gives to others, I feel good about it. Just a year ago I went to the Cook Islands in the South Pacific, where a Global Volunteers project was helping to teach children to read. And I've found ways to contribute to research or administrative needs when I've gone to Moscow on library exchanges or volunteering in Hungary.*

Through her travels, Jean has formed friendships that have resulted in connections around the world, leading to cross-generational relationships still sustained in New Zealand, the Middle East, and Morocco.

Like Jean, Thelma has also found that turning vacation time into work opportunities has proved more satisfying than being a tourist. As an Earthwatch volunteer she was able to help save the giant clam in Tonga, assist on an archaeological expedition in Turkey, and preserve ancient mosaics in a museum in Carthage, Tunisia. Each of the Earthwatch teams comprised ten to twelve members ranging widely in age. Interaction with people ranging from teens to seventies on projects requiring the contribution of each team member greatly enhanced the pleasure of seeing new parts of the world. Their shared purpose obliterated the divisions that age sometimes seems to create.

Pat H of Philadelphia, Pennsylvania, took her thirteen-year-old grandson with her to work at St. Dorcas Orphanage in Kenya, fulfilling a promise to each of four sibling grandchildren that each would travel with her when they reached their teens. Pat was sixty-eight at the time.

I had worked at a mobile health clinic in Mali as a volunteer. And while I feel Africa is a second home for me, the idea of a posh safari does not hold the same appeal as it might have done when I was younger. I have reached a point at which I really prefer to make a contribution if I can, and I wanted to give Drew the opportunity to see a very different life from his own, especially since I had told him when he was six and loved animals that I'd take him on a safari when he was older.

I found a volunteer opportunity in Kenya on the Internet and so we went. Handling lost luggage problems and plane changes in Brussels were all new to Drew—and so was his surprise that Grandma didn't take care of everything herself. But he rose to every occasion—great experience for him. When we got to the orphanage, bringing paper, pencils, crayons, books, inflatable soccer balls and pumps, and so on, we were given no instructions, just a tour of the place, which was very poor, the bunks where we would sleep, and classrooms. We soon figured out that he related well to the younger children and I did better with the teens and decided we'd work our own way. He's a very good artist and drew pictures to facilitate teaching English vocabulary as they taught him Swahili—and he played soccer with the other kids. Each of us bonded really closely with another individual. And he never complained about the very different food.

We were able to go on a safari to see the animals over a weekend—definitely not five-star!—and to visit a Masai village, where I was happy to see Drew join in the welcoming dance without self-consciousness. Riding in the local conveyances in Nairobi, where strangers might sit on our laps unbidden and someone thrust a hand through my open window to grab my camera (unsuccessfully), gave him a glimpse of third-world urban life. And at the end of our stay we visited an Indian family in Nairobi whose relative in Philadelphia had asked us to contact. They not only invited us to stay but took us to their temple and to a Hindu celebration.

I'm sure neither of us will ever forget this experience. Drew has the book he and his mother made when we got back. His ability to adjust to and enjoy every experience made me realize I need not cast a critical eye on how his parents are raising my grand-children!

Surely this cross-generational and multicultural adventure will have long-ranging effects in many lives, especially grandmother's and grandson's. What memories!

A YOUNG PERSON BURSTS THE BUBBLE

When **Benita Cooper**, a busy architect in her mid-twenties, living in Philadelphia, called her grandmother in Seattle to say hello, she had no idea that this would plant the seed for a cross-genera-tional program and community that is flourishing five years later, reaching more people than she can count. Benita had only in-tended to connect with family and practice her Cantonese, which was getting rusty since she had left Hong Kong at twelve. That first call began a regular weekly conversation.

My grandmother's stories, which no one in the family knew ("No one asks,"she told me.) transported me to the Chinese village where she was born, to an earlier Hong Kong, where she survived World War II and raised eleven children, and the Seattle suburb where she lives now. Her stories and our friend-ship made me realize how important it is to keep memories alive across generations and how much it means to listen and be listened to.

On her own, Benita went to a senior center not far from her office and asked whether she might meet with senior members for an hour each week, just to allow them to tell their stories and to listen. She provided writing materials for those who would like to write and then read what they had written to each other, thinking to offer them the prompt "The Best Day of My Life (So Far)," among others. She found, however, that the joy of expressing themselves, sharing their thoughts and feelings freely and without criticism, and developing a sense of community was virtually instantaneous. The prompt was not needed, but the name for the project remained. The first small group became the nucleus of a program that still includes a physical meeting with Benita every week for about a dozen or so writers, some of whom dictate to volunteer recorders if needed.

An unbreakable bond developed between the seniors and Benita. Soon volunteers, ranging in age from teens to eighty, were attracted to "The Best Day of My Life (So Far)." Just about anyone at any age who visits says, "How can I be of help?" With volunteers and advisors contributing time and skills and Benita's inspired leadership, today the website, The Best Day of My Life (So Far) reaches thousands of visitors, and the program is providing a model for widespread replication beyond all borders.

At a young age, Benita recognized that the value of her own relationship with her grandmother could serve as way to open communication across generations as well as across other cultural divisions. In acting on this recognition, she is providing the example for improving mental health and social problems affecting many neighborhoods and families today. And it all started with a phone call across the miles and the generations.

We asked **Sharon B**, who lives on Longboat Key, Florida, how she feels about living in a town populated mostly by retirees. She told us that it is very important for her to involve herself beyond this community.

I need to be engaged in the world. It's not enough to live in this beautiful place with very smart, affluent people. I know there's a world out there where people don't look like me, speak foreign languages, have different skin tones, other life experiences. I need to have diversity in my life in order to feel whole. I moved here from New York City, which is probably more engagement in the world than most people can tolerate. But I loved it. I loved the fact that every street is different, that many people speak languages I couldn't even identify, much less speak. I loved the chaos, the dynamism, the energy. Circumstances beyond my control required me to make this move.

Sharon, you don't seem to allow "circumstances" to limit your vision. You don't take on projects halfway. Having relatives in Israel, I know you've traveled there many, many times. Tell me why you decided to take on the serious issue of Israeli-Palestinian conflict and how you managed to reach women on a personal level.

By training I'm a mediator and have been on many missions in the Middle East, trying to find common ground in that intense conflict between Arab and Israeli women. It isn't as if I'm a part of a formal negotiating team. At least on the Israeli side, there have never been any women on the negotiating team. Maybe it's a little known fact, but for the past thirty years, Israeli and Palestinian women have been meeting regularly. They've been in dialogue. They can't solve all the problems, but at least they have been speaking and identifying some of the problems. They don't always agree, but they are willing to talk to each other.

I have found that Palestinian women, as an oppressed people, publicly put on a united front. Privately, they acknowledge the government can be unjust or unfair, as do the Israelis. There are also Palestinian and Israeli men who are very courageous, operating under the radar. Parents on both sides who have lost children in bombings are empathetic toward each other and participate in organizations on both sides who help each other.

I went with mostly non-Jews from Seattle called Compassion-ate Listening, which is a group that trains you how to listen to people's stories. We were welcomed into homes and offices on both sides, Palestinian and Israeli. It was a stunning experi-ence for me. I visited a Palestinian refugee camp and almost didn't get out when it was closed for the day by the IDF (Israe-li Defense Forces).

It was very courageous of you to visit a Palestinian refugee camp. When you are in the Middle East, do you feel wel-come by both Palestinian and Israeli women? What was your actual work?

My work there was to enable Palestinian and Israeli women to meet with each other as peers. That human interaction, wheth-er as peer groups or interest groups or ways to get people to know each other makes such a difference. When people have relationships, they are more likely to get along. When we live in fear and intimidation, it reduces our options and destroys opportunities.

I also worked as an executive director of an organization that supports a community, Neve Shalom/Wahat al-Salam, The Oa-sis of Peace, in a village of about fifty Palestinian Israeli and Jewish-Israeli families that lived together. They have a pri-mary and secondary school, education is bilingual, and the faculty binational. Life is challenging because they face daily the issues of national identity. Because they live in close quar-ters on a personal level, they have overcome issues of mistrust. They know that for each to survive, they have to get along, that neither nation is going to disappear. They are humanitarian, giving service and aid to people in need. Some are spiritual, some are not. But there are no fanatics there. No room for that.

I joined UN Women, which is an organization that I now chair because it is one of the few places in Sarasota where I meet women who aren't like me. It's another way of touching the rest of the world. Not only is the mission to be concerned about

*the rights and status of women globally, but the people who are
involved in this organization are a diverse group of people,
diverse in age, ethnicity, race, income, education. And we're all
equals.*

Sharon's involvement in the world never stops. Her curiosity is
insatiable. She is always foraging in new places for the unexpected
to satisfy her need to discover. What's next, Sharon?

When we interviewed **Mauriel H** of Philadelphia, Pennsylvania, we asked for her take on the safety of life surrounded by
contemporaries. We knew her opinion would be strong.

*My interests lie in a landscape that is wider than that of most
of my contemporaries. After I retired, I decided to join the
Peace Corps. I went to Lithuania for two years. I regret to say
that the only thing I can do is teach, so that's what I did.
Lithuania was getting out from under the Russian thumb after
the breakup of the USSR, so English, being considered an
international language, became the language of choice. There
was a huge demand for people to learn English. I worked for
the Labor Bureau, which was an agency that found jobs for
people. In order to find jobs as au pairs, waiters, store clerks,
tour guides—anything that required interface with tourists—
people had to learn English. These jobs were very coveted as
the former soviet socialist republics became independent.
There also was a strong push for children to learn English,
which I taught in kindergarten through twelfth-grade schools.
Another interesting part of my work in Lithuania was training
teachers who had been educated in village schools.*

*Actually, I have very few friends. Only one, really. My involve-
ment with people is as a part of all my volunteer activities. I
don't do social things just for the sake of being social. I don't
like to talk about painting my nails and other things that many
women like to talk about. That's all so trivial. And I can't bear
all the greeting each other and hugging each other. So much of
it is superficial, and I don't like it!*

The people I've met through volunteering are my friends. I teach English to foreigners who come from Central and South America, Japan, China, Africa—all over the world. I used to tutor at the Y, but when that venue was no longer available, I decided to teach in my home. They come from diverse backgrounds, jobs of all sorts, and varied educational levels. I get to know my students and their families well. When I travel to foreign countries, I sometimes visit their families. I also work at the central city library as a guide.

Overall, Mauriel finds much satisfaction in life. She makes sure to keep in touch with a wider world through her multicultural and multigenerational volunteer activities. Her choices ensure those kinds of contact. Her choices are not just to keep busy, but to be productive.

Some of the people we interviewed have told of the satisfaction in the different kind of travel available as they age. We asked **Thelma G**, in her nineties, about the "senior bubble." She has been on thirty-five cruises and visited ninety countries, usually going alone or in a group without a personal companion:

I've reached the point where I prefer to repeat a particular trip. For example, I love the cruise that takes you through the Panama Canal. People are always lovely—friendly and interesting. I just need to get to the airport in San Francisco and fly to San Diego. Someone from the cruise line meets me and gets me to the ship. Now that I find it hard to hear when I'm in a large group, I can still enjoy the lectures because I've heard it all before! I always bring a beaded black dress that belonged to my aunt (over a hundred years ago), a feathered band for my hair, and a long cigarette holder. On masquerade night, I go as a madam!

I'm finding that although physical travel has become somewhat more difficult, though fortunately not impossible, my real journey is an inner one. Not just through memory, though I do

> *some of that, but inwardly. I never used to understand when my contemporaries spoke of "finding themselves" when we were young, but now I do. It really does happen—learning who you are. And I find this very satisfying. I don't dwell on the mistakes I've made or the sadness of loss. And it does help to occasionally be with younger people, but frankly, I'm finding my own world is okay.*

We started this chapter with the thesis that *temptation* and *opportunity* are two main reasons that many seniors tend to enclose themselves in a bubble peopled by their contemporaries: the temptation to remain in a comfort zone and the lack of opportunity to interact with younger people in meaningful ways. For the women in this chapter, however, the temptation to just sit back and retire comfortably with their age peers is not an option. As one woman told us, she actually sleeps better and longer when she is "too busy with a meaningful task that has a deadline." The women in this chapter are also actively seeking opportunities to reach past their contemporaries into the wider world.

Gale needs to learn new skills as library science changed. So she did! Chiqui, Thelma, and Mauriel need to explore frontiers far afield from the comfort and safety of home and age peers. So they went! Blanche needs to pass on her passion for music to the next generations. So she does! The knowledge that the world can be improved in many ways triggered their decisions to do something about it, not just sit back and whine about how bad things are. These women have the curiosity, the interest, the courage, and the determination to set off on unfamiliar paths and continue to make important contributions to humanity. These women are not patronized. They are respected.

If you're in the bubble, make it dance.

11

FINALE

A Gathering of the Wisdom We Find in Each Other

For the unlearned, old age is winter; for the learned it is the season of the harvest.

—The Talmud

Dear ElderChicks and Boomers:

Is this really a "guide," and if so, how? You, who appear in this book, are the guides. You are the role models. You are showing the way. You, of course, are living according to your own *inner* guide. Barbara S, one of the women you met earlier, says she feels quite sure that spiritually, we have inner voices telling us what to do: we just have to listen. Our own inner voices find echoes and expansion when we listen to each other. Sometimes those other voices confirm what we know; sometimes they make us wince when they reflect attitudes or opinions we realize we need to shed. Growing old and growing up are not necessarily the same thing.

Guidebooks are usually written by experts. We well remember meeting a brilliant young researcher at Cambridge University in England who was studying and writing about how children learn phonics. We asked casually whether the scholar had ever actually taught a child. The answer was "No." This did not mean that her work would not be valuable or that she would be less able to design good instructional materials, but it would differ significantly from what an experienced teacher who teaches children all the time could tell us. Similarly, we are learning more every day from scientific research about aging; but for the most part, people who are living the experience are the experts we wanted to find. They—that is, you—would be our guides to the retirement years of today's senior woman. And you have not disappointed us.

WHAT WE FOUND

When we started this book three years ago, we often found ourselves recounting stories of the extraordinary women we were meeting and interviewing. Responses were in two categories. Overwhelmingly, listeners found the women they heard about to be inspiring and wanted to know more. But a small minority said, "Please, don't tell me about women who are happy, making it work, or achieving something. It only makes me feel inadequate."

Everyone we've met and learned about, with rare exceptions, could have come to that conclusion. No one reaches maturity, let alone advanced age, without challenges that could knock anyone off her feet. What becomes evident when we look at what the women in this book have to tell us is that the long view matters in the end, that most people realize that anyone could have been stopped in her tracks by any of the crises that abound in life: loss, separation, illness, abandonment, divorce, financial insecurity, deep disappointments in others and ourselves.

OUR TEACHERS, OUR PEERS

As we allow ourselves to continue to grow, however, we find our best teachers to be among our peers and ourselves. When we were very young, the world of aging seemed like a foreign country instead of the exciting place it turns out to be—full of new ideas, healthy reflection and self-awareness, and determination to make the most of the gift of years we're living and of this moment. It turns out that many people are making the most of this time in more ways than we expected.

As we mentioned in chapter 1, some asked, "Why only write about women?" We had answers: in our age group, women are the larger, faster-growing part of our society. Furthermore, women have experienced a profound role change following the 1960s, as a result of the work of Betty Friedan, Gloria Steinem, and other doyens of the women's movement. Many women were forever transformed: their expectations, their reach, their influence, their empowerment became the genesis of today's senior woman.

And as we think about all we've learned in our interviews, Lunch and Listen sessions, and conversations at senior centers, we've been struck by something we rarely asked directly but that underlies so much in the life of women at every stage of life: the role of friends and the bond of friendship, which for many is every bit as strong as the bonds of family—and for some even stronger. We found willingness, indeed eagerness to share observations, ideas, memories, fears, hopes, and deep feelings not only in women we already knew but in those we had known only for a moment. Where does that come from? It's definitely a woman thing! Until proven otherwise, the assumption is we are friends. It was a smart man, Rudyard Kipling, who observed,

> The Colonel's Lady an' Judy O'Grady
> Are sisters under their skins.

WE SHARE OUR SISTERHOOD

With age, we found, for women doing our senior act well, the trappings of privilege and the burdens of responsibility give way to common realities about our own mortality and inner journeys. Whether rich or poor, on Easy Street or in the land of hard knocks, the concerns and aspirations of fulfilled senior women strike a common chord. We all want respect, love, freedom, to find our place in the world, and to continue to grow and flourish. We who are finding the most satisfaction on our senior class trip seem to share, in addition to common realities, common attributes.

We face life with perspective. Having lived through so much pain and joy, we seem to know what is really important and what should be let go. We are flexible, are like the willow that bends rather than the oak that breaks. We are resilient, being able to pick ourselves up, dust ourselves off, and keep looking forward. We open our minds to fresh ideas and are more willing to accept change. We have compassion for the imperfections of others because we have become more tolerant of (not just giving lip service to) human frailties. We face life with humor rather than bitterness, having learned not to take ourselves too seriously to have fun. We are not so self-absorbed that we shut out the rest of the world. And from our learning, our wisdom, and our spirit, we have become strong. We have work to do. We have much more life to live. We are a force to be dealt with. We will leave our footprint. Legacy is on our minds.

ARE WE A NEW BREED?

We appear to be because we are in such a new landscape. Our mothers, aunts, and grandmothers needed and had the strength and determination that their times demanded, and they passed it on. But as they aged, so did their visibility decline—to a much greater extent than ours; the survivors were more likely to be shadow figures rather than active participants. The growth of our numbers means that we see so many more of us. Just watch the television commercials—if you can bear to. And notice that not every older woman's face on television is striving painfully to look young, as though aging were shameful.

Of course, it's not just our numbers and our potential as paying customers that is changing attitudes: it's our participation in communities, in workplaces, in public institutions, in active life that is having an impact. In particular, whenever we interact with younger people, we find more and more of them willing and even eager to listen—and not because we seem like quaint artifacts of an earlier time. Some of them listen because they see us as "elders" in experience and as role models. They see that age does not mean the end of personal growth, of change, of understanding who we are—of reflection, renewal, and acceptance. They begin to see that with good fortune and an open mind, they also can look forward to accepting a future where change is not necessarily the enemy. We are smart enough to know that our example counts so much more than what we say. Our ability to listen to younger people with respect rather than judgment begets their respect.

The women in this book are a diverse group indeed. Their very diversity reminds us of how much we share beneath all the outward trappings. Each has something we can learn from, just as you have. Your own experience has been your best teacher, yet you know how much you learn from others. That's why women care about other women's stories. There is a tension between the large picture and the small: keeping our perspective between our place in the universe as a grain of sand and being the center of our own. It is life's juggling act, and we are doing it as well as we possibly can.

You met Elena S earlier. We think her personal creed is a good way to end this book:

> While I can, I will.
> When I can't, I won't.
> But I'll be glad that I did when I could.

RECOMMENDED BOOKS

Alboher, Marci. *The Encore Career: How to Make a Living and Difference in the Second Half of Life*. New York: Workman, 2013.

Carstensen, Laura L. *A Long Bright Future*. New York: Broadway Books, 2009.

Fox, Elaine. *Rainy Brain, Sunny Brain: How to Retrain Your Brain to Overcome Pessimism and Achieve a More Positive Outlook*. New York: Basic, 2012.

Freedman, Marc. *The Big Shift: Navigating the New Stage beyond Midlife*. New York: Public Affairs, 2012.

Gianturco, Paola. *Grandmother Power: A Global Phenomenon*. Brooklyn: powerHouse Books, 2012.

Gross, Jane. *A Bittersweet Season: Caring for Our Aging Parents—and Ourselves*. New York: Vintage, 2012.

Levine, Suzanne Braun. *Fifty Is the New Fifty: Ten Life Lessons for Women in Second Adulthood*. New York: Viking Adult, 2009.

Perls, Thomas T., and Margery Hutter Silver. *Living to 100*. New York: Basic Books, 1999.

Roelofs, Lois Hoitenga. *Caring Lessons: A Nursing Professor's Journey of Faith and Self*. Sisters, OR: Deep River Books, 2010.

Walter, Carolyn Ambler. *The Loss of a Life Partner: Narratives of the Bereaved*. New York: Columbia University Press, 2003.

RECOMMENDED ORGANIZATIONS

Coming of Age: www.comingofage.org

Earthwatch Institute: www.earthwatch.org

Encore Careers: www.encore.org

Global Volunteers: www.globalvolunteers.org

Road Scholars: www.roadscholar.org (Elder Hostel, Inc.)

The Best Day of My Life (So Far): www.bestdayofmylifesofar.org

The Transition Network: Embracing Change after Fifty: the-transitionnetwork.org

ACKNOWLEDGMENTS

The New Senior Woman has been a transformative experience for us, mainly because of the women whose stories appear and the many young women who responded so enthusiastically to the idea of a book that provides models for them to think about. During the past three years, we have met many women who would otherwise not have crossed our paths, women whose stories have compelled us to reflect on our own lives as well as theirs. To them we say thank you for opening your hearts to us and opening our minds to yours.

To our blogmeister, Tory Bers, we are grateful for all her work in the creation of our blog, ElderChicks.com, which enlarged our community and, we hope, the community of women who found us. We were babes in the woods when it came to blogging and Facebook. Tory graciously put up with our rather steep learning curve.

Deep appreciation goes to the YoungerChicks and Younger-Dudes: Barbara's adult grandchildren: Duncan, Alex, Carla, Elisette, Ian, Daniel, and Yonatan—as well as Thelma's teen-age grandchildren Jacob and Emma—for their ever-present interest, support, and technological help, and for keeping us in their lives. Extra-special appreciation goes to Emma Bers, who created our logo. We are amazed that at the ripe old age of twelve, she was able to capture the essence of who we are and what we are trying to do.

We are grateful to our family for their honest feedback and valuable suggestions as the book progressed: Thelma's daughters Andrea and Tory and son-in-law Gerson; Barbara's daughters Jane and Wendy, daughter-in-law Virginia, son Peter, son-in-law Sapir, and Wendy's partner Ivor. They were our biggest fans.

And then there are our husbands. We always hung on Thelma's husband Harvey's words about all the facets and issues of authoring a book. He was our severest critic and our strongest cheering section. Unfortunately, Barbara's husband Dan did not live to see the publication of *The New Senior Woman*. But we can still hear him say, as he often did, "You can't be working very hard. You're laughing too much!"

Our thanks to our agent, Anne G. Devlin of the Max Gartenberg Literary Agency, for her enthusiasm. When she read our proposal, she told us that these are the things she and her friends are all talking about. And thanks also to Suzanne Staszak-Silva, our editor at Rowman & Littlefield, for all her help. We hope her mom enjoys this book. Melissa McNitt has been a most patient production editor; we deeply appreciate her help.

And finally, we want to acknowledge each other, without whom *The New Senior Woman* would never have happened. We both agree there is no one else we could have worked with. Positive and negative feedback was easily and honestly given. We were in perfect synchrony with each other's thoughts, writing styles, and what we wanted to accomplish. Our friendship has strengthened immeasurably as a result of this journey.

NOTES

1. MY MOTHER'S SENIOR YEARS WERE SO DIFFERENT FROM MINE

1. Projections for 2010 through 2050 are from table 12. "Projections of the Population by Age and Sex for the United States: 2010 to 2050" (NP2008-T12), Population Division, US Census Bureau, release date August 14, 2008. This table was compiled by the US Administration on Aging using the census data noted. United States Census Bureau, International Data Base, US Department of Commerce.

2. US Centers for Disease Control and Prevention, table 18, "Life expectancy at birth, at age 65, and at age 75 by sex, race, and Hispanic origin: United States (selected years 1900–2010)," 2012, available at www.cdc.gov/nchs/hus/contents2012.htm#018.

2. SO NOW I'M RETIRED

1. Lucia Blinn, "This Is Not Working," in *Passing for Normal* (Chicago: First Flight Books, 2004), 9.

2. Vincent J. Felitti et al., "Relationship of Childhood Abuse and Household Dysfunction to Many of the Leading Causes of Death in Adults: The Adverse Childhood Experiences (ACE) Study," *American Journal of Preventive Medicine* 14 (1998): 245–58.

3. Lois Hoitenga Roelofs, *Caring Lessons: A Nursing Professor's Journey of Faith and Self* (Sisters, OR: Deep River Books, 2010).

3. I FINALLY HAVE MY FREEDOM AND INDEPENDENCE

1. Marylen Oberman, *Crash Course: Life Lessons That Got Me Back on My Feet* (Ann Arbor: Huron River Press, 2006).
2. Eldering: Wisdom in Action, website of the Eldering Institute, http://www.elderinginstitute.com. The Eldering Institute is located at 8733 Rosario Place NW, Bainbridge Island, WA, 98110.
3. Charles Durrett, *The Senior Cohousing Handbook: A Community Approach to Independent Living*, 2nd ed. (Gabriola Island, Canada: New Society Publishers, 2009).

6. I CAN'T USE MY COMPUTER—OR KNIT OR ROLLERBLADE

1. Christina Bonnington, "Seniors, Women Embracing Tablets, E-Readers," *Wired*, August 29, 2011.
2. Ibid.
3. Mary Madden, "Older Adults and Social Media," Pew Research Center's Internet & American Life Project Report, August 27, 2010.

7. WE LAUGH ABOUT OUR "SENIOR MOMENTS"

1. G. O. Einstein and M. A. McDaniel, *Memory Fitness: A Guide for Successful Aging* (New Haven: Yale University Press, 2004).
2. E. A. Stine-Morrow, "The Dumbledore Hypothesis of Cognitive Aging," *Current Directions in Psychological Science* 16 (2007): 295–99; C. Hertzog, A. F. Kramer, R. S. Wilson, and U. Lindenberger, "Enrichment Effects on Adult Cognitive Development: Can the Functional Capacity of Older Adults Be Preserved and Enhanced?" *Psychological Science in the Public Interest* 9 (2009): 1–65; "10 Research-Proven Tips

for a Better Memory," *HEALTHbeat* newsletter, Harvard Health Publications, May 10, 2006, http://www.health.harvard.edu/healthbeat/HEALTHbeat_051006.htm#art1.

3. G. L. Bowman et al., " Nutrient Biomarker Patterns, Cognitive Function, and MRI Measures of Brain Aging," Neurology 78 (2012) : 241 – 49 .

9. SEPARATION AND LOSS ARE FACTS
OF LIFE

1. Carolyn Ambler Walter, *The Loss of a Life Partner: Narratives of the Bereaved* (New York: Columbia University Press, 2003).

10. SOMETIMES I FEEL SAFEST IN MY
SENIOR BUBBLE

1. Paola Gianturco, *Grandmother Power: A Global Phenomenon* (Brooklyn: powerHouse Books, 2012).

BIBLIOGRAPHY

Blinn, Lucia. "This Is Not Working." In *Passing for Normal*, 9. Chicago: First Flight Books, 2004.

Bonnington Christina. "Seniors, Women Embracing Tablets, E-Readers." Wired Magazine, August 29, 2011.

Bowman, G. L., L. C. Silbert, D. Howieson, H. H. Dodge, M. G. Traber, B. Frei, J. A. Kaye, J. Shannon, and J. F. Quinn. "Nutrient Biomarker Patterns, Cognitive Function, and MRI Measures of Brain Aging." Neurology 78 (2012): 241–49.

Durrett, Charles. *The Senior Cohousing Handbook: A Community Approach to Independent Living*. 2nd ed. Gabriola Island, Canada: New Society Publishers, 2009.

Einstein, G. O, and M. A. McDaniel. *Memory Fitness: A Guide for Successful Aging*. New Haven: Yale University Press, 2004.

Felitti, Vincent J., Robert F. Anda, Dale Nordenberg, David F. Williamson, Alison M. Spitz, Valerie Edwards, Mary P. Koss, and James S. Marks. "Relationship of Childhood Abuse and Household Dysfunction to Many of the Leading Causes of Death in Adults: The Adverse Childhood Experiences (ACE) Study." *American Journal of Preventive Medicine* 14 (1998): 245–58. http://www.ajpmonline.org/article/S0749-3797%2898%2900017-8/fulltext.

Gianturco, Paola. *Grandmother Power: A Global Phenomenon*. Brooklyn: powerHouse Books, 2012.

A Guide to Alzheimer's Disease. Special Health Report. Harvard Health Publications, 2012. http://www.health.harvard.edu/special_health_reports/a-guide-to-alzheimers-disease.

Hertzog, C., A. F. Kramer, R. S. Wilson, and U. Lindenberger. "Enrichment Effects on Adult Cognitive Development: Can the Functional Capacity of Older Adults Be Preserved and Enhanced?" *Psychological Science in the Public Interest* 9 (2009): 1–65.

Madden, Mary. "Older Adults and Social Media." Pew Research Center's Internet & American Life Project Report, August 27, 2010. http://www.pewinternet.org/Reports/2010/Older-Adults-and-Social-Media/Report.aspx.

Oberman, Marylen. *Crash Course: Life Lessons That Got Me Back on My Feet*. Ann Arbor, MI: Huron River Press, 2006.

Roelofs, Lois Hoitenga. *Caring Lessons: A Nursing Professor's Journey of Faith and Self*. Sisters, OR: Deep River Books, 2010.

Selman, James C. "Eldering: Wisdom in Action." Eldering Institute, 2008. http://www.elderinginstitute.com/resources/articles/eldering.

Stine-Morrow, E. A. "The Dumbledore Hypothesis of Cognitive Aging." *Current Directions in Psychological Science* 16 (2007): 295–99.

"10 Research-Proven Tips for a Better Memory." *HEALTHbeat* newsletter. Harvard Health Publications, May 10, 2006. http://www.health.harvard.edu/healthbeat/HEALTHbeat_051006.htm#art1.

US Census Bureau. Table 12, "Projections of the Population by Age and Sex for the United States: 2010 to 2050 (NP2008-T12)." Population Division, August 14, 2008.

US Centers for Disease Control and Prevention. Table 18, "Life expectancy at birth, at age 65, and at age 75 by sex, race, and Hispanic origin: United States, selected years 1900–2010)," 2012. Available at www.cdc.gov/nchs/hus/contents2012.htm#018.

Walter, Carolyn Ambler. *The Loss of a Life Partner: Narratives of the Bereaved*. New York: Columbia University Press, 2003.

Werner, Carrie A. "The Older Population: 2010." 2010 Census Brief. US Census Bureau, November 2011. http://www.census.gov/prod/cen2010/briefs/c2010br-09.pdf.

READERS' GUIDE: QUESTIONS FOR DISCUSSION

1. How is your life different from your mother's? How are your expectations for your senior years different from hers? What, if any, options do you have that are different from hers? Whatever your answer, do you regard this as a positive or a negative?

2. You have probably planned financially for your retirement years. What plans have you made for your emotional and spiritual well-being? If you are already in the senior stage of your life, how has your life-style changed? What adjustments are needed to make this stage successful?

3. What are your thoughts about our society's attitudes about aging? Would you like to see attitudes change? If so, what changes would you like to see and how would you go about effecting those changes?

4. What are your feelings about a second career in retirement? What are your feelings about volunteer work? How do you find purpose and meaning in your life?

5. In what ways are your new freedom and independence as rewarding (or not) as you had expected? Now that your

responsibilities have changed do you feel liberated or irrelevant?

6. Have your attitudes toward possessions and material goods changed? How about toward fashion and makeup? Manners and values? Morals and standards?

7. What are your attitudes toward your children: their lifestyles, families, partners, the way they raise their children, your place in their lives, their place in yours? How do you express approval, disapproval, or concerns?

8. How do you keep in touch with the world around you? How hard do you try to communicate with people many years your junior or senior? How important are intergenerational contacts in your life? What do you do to make them happen?

9. If you are part of the sandwich generation – caught between adult children and aging parents—what do you see as the issues? Their dependency? Your responsibility?

10. What's the next new thing you're planning to learn? What talents and interests are you continuing to develop?

11. As a consequence of reading this book, or of participating in this discussion, what changes, if any, in your life might you consider? For each chapter, participants can also discuss individual stories which they found particularly compelling.

ABOUT THE AUTHORS

Barbara M. Fleisher, EdD, is a retired professor of education. She is the author of many articles in professional juried journals and has presented her research at national and international conferences. She has made presentations and conducted many workshops for and about women in their sixties and beyond and has interviewed hundreds of women about their concerns as they face new challenges in this stage in their lives.

Thelma Reese, EdD, retired professor of English and of education, created the advisory council for Hooked on Phonics and was its spokesperson in the 1990s. In that role and as director of the Mayor's Commission on Literacy for the City of Philadelphia, she appeared frequently on television and hosted a cable show in Philadelphia. Together, she and Barbara M. Fleisher created and maintain the www.ElderChicks.com blog. She writes the monthly "Family" column for Right SideWire, and she and Barbara appear weekly on the *Armstrong Williams* show on Sirius Radio as he plumbs the wisdom of the "ElderChicks."

Dick Goldberg is the national director of Coming of Age, the age 50-plus civic engagement initiative working in thirty communities. In his previous career as a playwright and screenwriter, among the works he authored was the off-Broadway drama *Family Business*, which ran in New York for over a year, was produced in regional theaters around the world, and was the basis for his becoming a Guggenheim Fellow.